THE GREAT BRITISH BUCKET LIST

RICHARD MADDEN

THE GREAT BRITISH BUCKET LIST

🌿 National Trust

Published by National Trust Books
An imprint of HarperCollins Publishers
1 London Bridge Street
London SE1 9GF
www.harpercollins.co.uk

HarperCollins Publishers
Macken House, 39/40 Mayor Street Upper,
Dublin 1, D01 C9W8, Ireland

Volume © National Trust Books, 2019
Text © Richard Madden, 2019
Illustrations by Sara Mulvanny/agencyrush.com 2019

The moral rights of the author have been asserted.

The contents of this publication are believed correct at the time of printing.
Nevertheless, the publisher can accept no responsibility for errors or
omissions, changes in the detail given or for any expense or loss
thereby caused.

ISBN: 9781911358732

A catalogue record for this book is available from the British

20 19 18 17 16 15 14 13 12

Reproduction by Rival Colour Ltd, UK
Printed and bound in India

If you would like to comment on any aspect of this book, please
contact us at the above address or national.trust@harpercollins.co.uk

National Trust publications are available at National Trust shops
or online at nationaltrustbooks.co.uk

MIX
Paper | Supporting
responsible forestry
FSC™ C007454

Contents

Introduction

Buckets are contradictory objects. On the one hand, they are among the most mundane of everyday items. On the other, they have acquired a semi-mystical alternative existence, first as a door marked 'Exit' between this world and the next, and secondly as a receptacle for our dreams of must-do life experiences. The latter all to be completed before that inevitable wayward foot finally makes contact with the former.

You don't have to look far to find books and travel features in newspapers and magazines that contain 'Bucket List' suggestions for visiting far-flung parts of the globe. Often, they are combined with adrenaline pumping experiences. Riding horses through the African bush, long-distance cycling epics across the Far East, or crewing ocean-going yachts around the world, to name but a few.

I've been lucky enough to experience many of these kinds of adventures myself. As an adventure travel writer and editor for more than 20 years, I've had my fair share of death-defying experiences from skydiving, paragliding and bungee jumping to sailing, diving and white-water rafting. Not to mention a fair few in between with feet, wheels or hooves planted firmly on terra firma.

Despite of this (or perhaps because of it!) I was delighted when the National Trust asked me if I would write a book about the most compelling places to visit, and experiences to be enjoyed, on home turf. But this time without the necessity of leaping out of a plane or testing my survival skills in winter in the Cairngorms.

While I have hugely enjoyed exploring the far-flung parts of our amazing planet, I have also become increasingly aware of just how much there is in the UK to discover in a more relaxed frame of mind (and body). Our history and heritage, our buildings and gardens, our wildlife, ancient monuments, music, art, festivals, traditions and, of course, our great and beautiful outdoors.

We agreed to divide the book into sections that covered examples of all the above. From then on, it was up to me. As a Fellow of the Royal Geographical Society, a Member of the Institute of Tourist Guiding (Blue Badge Guide) and a travel writer, I had my own bucket of experiences to fall back on. For the rest, there followed some enjoyable weeks of research scurrying around the UK discovering yet more of our seemingly endless national treasures.

The problem, of course, was not what to include in our metaphorical bucket. But what not to include. Why, for example, include Westminster Abbey but not St Paul's Cathedral? Why Hadrian's Wall and not Bath's Roman Baths? Why the Helston Furry Dance and not Leicester's Diwali Festival? Inevitably, space is the primary answer, but also the desire not to repeat similar themes. I also wanted my choices to be based on personal experience, whether directly as a result of researching this book, or from previous knowledge.

We also wanted to ensure we covered a good selection of the classics (The Tower of London, Giant's Causeway, Stonehenge & Avebury) along with some lesser-known gems (Yorkshire Sculpture Park, Kielder Observatory, Down House – Darwin's Home) and some uniquely British experiences (a Spitfire flight, afternoon tea at the Ritz, eating fish & chips). The intention was to arrive at a list where there would always be possible additions, but definitively no surplus inclusions.

The result is a book that I am delighted to put my name to and which I hope will provide a source of both inspiration and information to all lovers of the UK. These are all magical destinations and experiences, all of which I can personally endorse as worthy of multiple visits. Enjoy the journey and may all your buckets be full ones!

BRITAIN'S UNMISSABLE HERITAGE

Windsor Castle

Ancestral home of British royalty

An Englishman's home may be his castle, but the castle of an English queen is also her home. And Windsor Castle is where Queen Elizabeth II, the longest-reigning monarch in British history, feels most at home. It is her official residence for a month over Easter and again for a week in June for Royal Ascot and the Order of the Garter ceremony. But, perhaps more significantly, Windsor is where she spends most of her private weekends.

She is not the first of our monarchs to call Windsor home. Over the castle's 950-year history, 40 kings and queens stretching back to Henry I (crowned in 1100) have spent significant periods of their reign here. Which is why many of the thousands of visitors who queue outside the castle walls every day in summer gaze up so hopefully at the flagstaff on the top of the Round Tower. If the Royal Standard is flying they know the Queen is in residence. Whether they will be invited into the private apartments for a cup of tea is another matter entirely.

Rebuilt in stone in the twelfth century to replace William the Conqueror's original wooden fortress, Windsor Castle oozes history from every brick, turret, chandelier and gold-plated clock. As well as the hundreds of paintings by Old Masters including Holbein, Rembrandt, Canaletto, van Dyke and Reynolds, the State Apartments include vast gilded reception rooms, painted ceilings, shining coats of armour, carved wooden furniture, gold and silver plate, sculpted marble mantelpieces, giant tapestries, and the ancient pikes, muskets and pistols of generations of royal guards. Even the bullet that killed Nelson at the Battle of Trafalgar is on display in its own silver locket.

The centerpiece of the State Apartments is St George's Hall. Its hammer-beam roof, the largest green-oak structure constructed since the Middle Ages, was rebuilt after the devastating 1992 fire, while its dining table seats 160 people and takes ten people two days to lay up for a state banquet. Around 18,000 bottles of wine are kept in the cellar and the whisking bowl in the Great Kitchen can hold up to 250 eggs at one time. Hardly surprising then that the kitchen clocks run five minutes fast to ensure that the food is never served late.

St George's Chapel, for many the highlight of a visit to Windsor, is the spiritual home of the Knights of the Order of the Garter, Britain's highest order of chivalry, founded by Edward III in 1348. It is considered by architectural historians to be one of the finest examples of English Perpendicular Gothic architecture in the land. In the quire, adjacent to the high altar, are the exquisitely carved, fifteenth-century wooden choir stalls with the banners, helms, crests and swords of the Garter Knights.

Eleven monarchs are buried in St George's Chapel, including Henry VIII in 1547, Charles I after his execution in 1649, and Queen Elizabeth II's father George VI in 1952, while unique historic treasures include the giant two-handed broadsword that belonged to Edward III. It has also witnessed many royal marriages, including that of Prince Harry to Meghan Markle in 2018. Home, after all, is where the heart is.

Stonehenge
& Avebury

Riddles from the Stone Age

It's one of the great rites of the British summer. At dawn on 21 June, as the sun rises over Stonehenge to usher in the summer solstice, thousands gather to welcome its first rays as it emerges on the longest day of the year. From the middle of the circle, the sun's orb can be seen rising between one of the surrounding trilithons above the Heel Stone. This outlying sarsen stone stands at the apex of what was once a ceremonial avenue leading into the centre of the circle from the nearby River Avon. Guiding the ritual celebrations are white-cloaked Druids, modern-day revivalists of the religious beliefs of the Celtic tribes that inhabited these shores before the arrival of the Romans.

'The wrong people facing the wrong way on the wrong day.' That's currently
the opinion of most leading archaeologists, citing the many recent discoveries
that are casting a new light on the question of who built the world-famous
monument and why. It's a riddle that has bemused antiquarians ever since
John Aubrey and William Stukeley pondered it in the seventeenth and
eighteenth centuries.

One thing is for sure, Stonehenge was built long before the arrival of the
Druids, the central circle being erected in about 2500BC. Evidence at nearby
Durrington Walls, where the builders of Stonehenge lived, suggests that the
huge feasts held around mid-winter point to sunset on the winter solstice as
the focus of the main annual ritual. The entrance of the ceremonial avenue
from the north-east and the more 'dressed' (polished) finish of the stones on this
side also indicate that the temple was oriented towards the winter, rather than
the summer, solstice.

Or perhaps not. Perhaps it was indeed a celestial observatory, an acoustic sound chamber or the centre of a healing cult. That it was once a cemetery and later became a healing site after the famous bluestones were transported all the way from the Preseli Hills in Wales has been proved beyond reasonable doubt. Or perhaps it was all of these things and more. The theories of the purpose of Stonehenge and the rituals that took place here are in a constant state of flux, often reflecting the preoccupations of each passing generation.

The same can be said of nearby Avebury which, John Aubrey wrote, did 'as much excell Stonehenge as a Cathedral does a parish church.' The central henge with its large circular bank and internal ditch is nearly 400 yards in diameter. This surrounds the world's largest stone circle – once made up of 98 standing stones – which, in turn, surrounds two more giant circles.

To the south are Silbury Hill and West Kennet Long Barrow. The former is the largest man-made prehistoric mound in Europe and was long thought to be the tomb of a tribal chieftain, a theory disproved after three major excavations. The estimated four million hours it took to construct must surely

have had some purpose, but this can still only be guessed at, making the Avebury landscape the most complex riddle of them all.

Our ancestors have handed down some enduring mysteries: the pyramids, the Easter Island statues, the Nazca Lines, the Mayan temples of Central America. For many, they are a doorway into the imagination and, for some, into Otherworlds and the meaning of existence. Perhaps, like all good riddles, the mystery will always be more fascinating than the solution.

The Tower of London

Great British time machine

Time machines don't all come in the shape of a police telephone box. While the TARDIS may be Dr Who's chosen method of reversing time's arrow, the Tower of London is a much more practical option. With the added advantage of being much more spacious – both inside and out.

So where in time shall we travel? What period of our national history would you like to visit? In the Tower you will find artefacts from every historic era going back to the Roman occupation of Britain in the first few centuries BC.

At the centre of it all is the famous White Tower, that monolithic fortress built by the Conqueror himself in 1078 not long after the Battle of Hastings. It was here, centuries later, that the bones of the ill-fated 'Princes in the Tower' were discovered, probably murdered on the orders of the villainous Richard, Duke of Gloucester, later Richard III.

It's true, there's plenty of gore. History's like that. It's hard not to gaze at Traitors' Gate, the waterside entrance where the condemned bade farewell to life and liberty, and not remember the fate of those such as Sir Thomas More who were imprisoned here. Or look at the carved name of Ambrose Rookwood, one of the conspirators in the Gunpowder Plot, later hanged, drawn and quartered. Not to mention the strange zodiac in the Salt Tower left behind by Hew Draper, a Bristol innkeeper accused of sorcery in 1561.

Nevertheless, standing at the site of the executioner's block, where tragic figures such as Anne Boleyn and Lady Jane Grey met their end, is more emotional than ghoulish. Today a sculpture of a glass pillow marks the spot, while the more brutal reminder of a wooden block and axe are preserved inside the walls of the tower. But, hey, chin up time-travellers, there's more to history than blood and guts. This is also the home of the Crown Jewels. If you

think stars glisten, you've obviously never seen the monarchy's collection of top-end bling. Diamonds are two a penny including one of the most famous of them all, the infamous Koh-i-Noor diamond set in the crown worn by Queen Elizabeth, the Queen Mother, at the coronation of George VI in 1937.

Less famous but equally fascinating is the twelfth-century 'Coronation Spoon', used by the Archbishop of Canterbury to anoint every new sovereign with oil since James I in 1603, and one of the few royal jewels to survive the English Civil War.

Time's whirligig also throws up some weird and wonderful costumes from the long-lost past. Most obvious are the Tudor-style uniforms of the Yeomen Warders, better known as 'Beefeaters', but on any day of the year you are likely to see Tower staff wearing a fabulous mix of outfits worthy of a time-traveller's most improbable imaginings from medieval peasants to Tudor royalty. And they beat T-shirts and trainers any day.

Look around and you will also see gazing out at you – from arches and hidden corners – the wire sculptures of the lions, leopards, elephants and even a polar bear that once occupied the Tower's menagerie and were housed here for more than 600 years until 1835.

And what of those famous ravens? One of the Tower's most enduring legends is that if they disappear the Tower, the monarchy and the country itself will be doomed. Hardly surprising then that there's a royal decree for keeping six (and one spare) under the protection of a Ravenmaster, one of the Yeoman Warders. So be careful to leave them be when you finally return to the London of the twenty-first century.

Westminster Abbey

Our national shrine

It is the mood of hushed reverence that is so immediately striking. A sense of history that is almost tangible. It is in the soaring Gothic arches, the masterly detail of the medieval stonemasons, the wood carvings on the sixteenth-century misericords, the side chapels and the altars, the transepts and the spires, the thrones and the altarpieces, the tombs and the memorials, the galleries and the cloisters. Above all it is in the flickering shadows of candles burning in remembrance.

It seems to flow from every corner and every pore of a building that feels like a living presence, remembering and celebrating the lives of kings and queens, prime ministers, statesmen, military heroes, scientists, poets, actors, artists, musicians, composers, engineers, the list goes ever on. And now, in the nave close to the graves of Newton and Darwin, lie the ashes of Stephen Hawking, interred in June 2018.

Just inside the Great West Door is the Tomb of the Unknown Soldier. For many visitors this is the most moving of all the tombs, which stretch back to the shrine of Edward the Confessor who founded Westminster Abbey in 1065. The significance of the Unknown Soldier cannot be overstated. He represents not only the heroism of the soldiers who never returned from the battlefields of the First World War but also the anonymity of true heroism everywhere. A sacred shrine to Everyman in the temple of the great and the good.

Historians of the kings and queens of England and Scotland and the religious wars, which have led to so much bloodshed over the centuries, may raise a wry smile at the democracy of death. The two daughters of Henry VIII, the one 'Bloody' Mary, a fervent Catholic, the other Elizabeth I, a Protestant, lie in the same tomb in the Henry VII chapel. It bears the epitaph: 'Partners

in throne and grave, here we sleep Elizabeth and Mary, sisters in hope of Resurrection'. In the opposite aisle is the marble tomb of the Catholic Mary, Queen of Scots, executed on Elizabeth I's orders in 1587.

And then there's the Coronation Chair in St George's Chapel, commissioned by Edward I in 1308 to hold the famous Stone of Scone, which has been used in 38 coronations. Its fame has also attracted some less well-known attention. One decidedly unroyal piece of graffiti reads: 'P. Abbott slept in this chair 5–6 July 1800'.

In 2018 the Abbey opened the galleries in the beautiful thirteenth-century triforium, more than 50ft above the floor of the nave. On the way up in the glass-curtain lift, the new Weston Tower has sweeping views over the Palace

of Westminster and the medieval Chapter House. Hidden away from the public gaze for more than 700 years, the triforium treasures include an effigy of Henry VII modelled on his death mask, and the *Liber Regalis*, a fourteenth-century guide to staging coronations and royal funerals that is still followed to this day.

The Abbey continues to make history and is rarely far from the centre of national consciousness. Visiting it is to make a pilgrimage to a national shrine whose modern history has included shared national experiences of both mourning and celebration, including the funeral of Diana, Princess of Wales, in 1997, and the audience of nearly a billion who watched the wedding of the Duke and Duchess of Cambridge in 2011.

Chatsworth House

A home fit for a duchess

One hundred and twenty-six rooms. Seventeen staircases. Half a mile of passageways. A roof the size of a football pitch. Chatsworth House is one of the largest and most palatial private houses in the land. Its 100-acre gardens are looked after by 20 full-time gardeners and display more than 70 stone sculptures. When viewed from the south, its 300-yard pond makes the house look like its floating on water. The house and garden receive over 650,000 visitors each year, with many more coming to enjoy the surrounding park.

But statistics like these tell only a small part of the story of a country seat in the heart of Derbyshire that has been home to the Dukes of Devonshire for nearly 500 years, passed down through 16 generations of the Cavendish

family. Since the Hollywood film *The Duchess* was released in 2008, Chatsworth has become famous for being the home of Georgiana, wife of the 5th Duke, a Spencer by birth and an ancestor of Diana, Princess of Wales.

Their stories have some startling parallels, most notably a passionate extra-marital love affair following a suffocating marriage involving a ménage à trois. She was also a political activist and a fashion icon. After the birth of a legitimate son and heir, Georgiana was banished from Chatsworth after running up huge debts due to her gambling addiction and becoming pregnant with her lover's child. A letter to her estranged son written in her own blood still survives, expressing her sadness that she may never see him again.

Even the story of her portrait, painted by Gainsborough in 1787, and showing her wearing a gargantuan black hat reflecting her larger-than-life personality, is the stuff of Chatsworth legend. Lost and then found in the home of an elderly schoolmistress it was later sold at Christie's only to be stolen by Adam Worth, the notorious 'Napoleon of Crime' and the inspiration behind Conan Doyle's James Moriarty, arch-enemy of Sherlock Holmes. In 1994, it finally returned to Chatsworth more than 200 years after it left.

Highlights? In a house of this magnitude and historical importance, the treasures on display are too many and too varied to do justice in a few short sentences. The Painted Hall is high on any list. First impressions count, not just for modern visitors but more importantly for the guests of the 1st Duke who created it in the seventeenth century. The vastness of the Hall, the brilliant colours of the painted ceiling, the numerous works of art, wall paintings, sculptures and the imposing staircase dominated by the bronze statue of Mercury are immediately striking.

Outside, the gardens have features from all six centuries of its development. The most famous is the Cascade, completed in 1696 fronted by the Baroque Cascade House temple and a fountain that sends water flowing down the steps below. Each step is different so the sound of the water changes as it descends. The water comes from the moorland above the house along a series of man-made streams and an aqueduct. One of the Duke's favourite party tricks was to turn on the jets hidden in the floor of the Cascade House, taking guests by surprise and soaking them in the process. They still work!

Cliveden House

Politics, parties and a notorious swimming pool

Sex, debauchery, politics, scandal, the English aristocracy. Now there's an intriguing story you can't ignore. And while we're about it, why not throw in one of the most beautiful, grand and elegant country houses in the land, a Grade I listed stately home perched high above the Thames in rural Buckinghamshire? It all adds up to charisma on an epic scale and Cliveden House is more than happy to be the beneficiary.

And what a compelling story it is. It all began – appropriately enough – with one of history's most rakish figures, namely George Villiers, the 2nd Duke of Buckingham. Villiers, who acquired the land during the reign of the 'Merry Monarch' Charles II, built a hunting lodge on his new estate to entertain his mistress and friends. But his penchant for beautiful women – most notably the wife of the Earl of Shrewsbury – eventually led to his fall from grace after he mortally wounded the Earl in a duel.

Cliveden's Golden Age began when it was bought by the fabulously wealthy American entrepreneur William Waldorf Astor in 1893. During the Astor era, the house was transformed into an eclectic mish-mash of pomp and circumstance combining furnishings and historic architectural features from all over Europe. The French Dining Room, for example, has preserved every last detail of a wood-panelled room from the Château d'Asnières near Paris, the hunting lodge of Louis XV's mistress, Madame de Pompadour.

After the First World War Nancy Astor, the first ever female MP, turned Cliveden into the epicentre of a social whirlwind on an international scale. As well as being home to her five children, the house was visited by royalty, politicians, literary giants and stars of the silver screen, including Charlie Chaplin, many of whom were photographed on the famous South Terrace looking out over the six-acre parterre, which is still one of the garden's most spectacular features.

But it was another scandal involving the rich and powerful for which Cliveden is primarily remembered. The year was 1961 and during the chill of the Cold War, Cliveden was basking in a sultry summer of sweltering heat. Cooling off in the now infamous outdoor pool – today the last remaining listed outdoor pool in England – was Christine Keeler, the 19-year-old mistress of a suspected Russian spy. Also in attendance was John Profumo, the Secretary of State for War. The affair that followed was instrumental in bringing down the Conservative government three years later.

Since 1985, Cliveden has been a five-star hotel ushering visitors into an environment of pure historical theatre surrounded by 375 acres of formal gardens and woodlands owned by the National Trust and open year-round. The hotel itself is furnished with antiques and original works of art while the rooms have handmade king-sized beds, high ceilings, gilt fireplaces and spectacular views over the gardens and estates. Its spa, hidden discretely away behind brick walls adorned with scented roses and lavender, is also home to the infamous Profumo swimming pool. Just don't mention the affair!

Portsmouth Historic Dockyard

Where Britannia rules the waves

Do you, after a glass or two too many, break into a raucous chorus of 'Rule Britannia' while watching the *Last Night of the Proms* on TV? If so, assuming you have not done so already, you must make a date to visit Portsmouth's Historic Dockyard in Hampshire. Your country expects...

There, as you stroll the quarterdeck of HMS *Victory* and find yourself on the exact spot where Nelson was mortally wounded by a sniper's bullet at 1.15pm on 21 October 1805, the hairs on the back of your neck will stand on end.

By now you will have learnt about the daring and revolutionary tactics Nelson employed at Trafalgar, attacking the enemy's straight defensive line in two perpendicular columns. His aim was to split the combined force of the French and Spanish navies and overcome his significant numerical disadvantage. To do so he placed both his flagship and himself in the firing line.

As you stroll below decks and see the cramped living quarters of the men who sailed the ship and fought this era-defining battle, you will find yourself imagining the smoke and noise, the shouts and screams of battle, the deafening roar of a close-quarter broadside. You will also see the very spot where Nelson died attended by the *Victory*'s surgeon, William Beatty.

Day-to-day living on a battleship is also brought vividly to life in the adjacent *Mary Rose* Museum, a Tudor time capsule in its own state-of-the-art exhibition space. Built on three deck-like floors around the hull of Henry VIII's flagship, it tells the story of how the *Mary Rose* capsized in July 1545 during the Battle of the Solent. The ship was engaging a French fleet of more than 200 ships at the time, considerably larger than the more famous Spanish Armada 43 years later. The exact reason for the disaster may never be known but was probably due to a combination of factors. In full view of the King, who was watching the battle from Southsea Castle, the *Mary Rose* made a sharp turning manoeuvre while its lower gunports were still open. At the same time a strong gust of wind caught its mainsail. Recent design adjustments may also have had a destabilising effect. The death toll was so high – only 35 of the 400 crew survived – because netting designed to stop enemy soldiers boarding the boat had been spread over the upper deck and the escaping crew were unable to swim clear.

More than 19,000 artefacts have been recovered from the wreck of the *Mary Rose*. These include cooking utensils, medical and musical instruments, shoes, clothing, chess pieces and even a nit comb complete with original Tudor head lice. The skeletons of a carpenter, the cook, a gunner, as well as several officers and archers have been reconstructed. 'Hatch', the skeleton of a mongrel dog, is a popular mascot for the museum and was most probably employed as the ship's ratter.

The *Victory* and the *Mary Rose* are the stars of an extensive dockyard site that includes other historic ships, museums, exhibitions spaces, restaurants and cafés.

Beaulieu National Motor Museum

Cars, monks, aristocrats... and spies

Jeremy Clarkson would make an unlikely monk, he makes no claims to be an aristocrat and he'd definitely make a lousy spy. Blending in is just not his forte. But petrolheads sometimes choose strange bedfellows and the 'World of Top Gear' exhibition at the Beaulieu Estate in the New Forest shares centre stage with all three. At the heart of it all is the National Motor Museum itself, founded in 1952 by the 3rd Baron Montagu. Elsewhere in the grounds are Palace House, the Montagu historic family home; Beaulieu Abbey, the ruins of a thirteenth-century Cistercian monastery; and, most intriguing of all, the Secret Army Exhibition telling the incredible story of Beaulieu's role as a training ground for 3,000 agents of the Special Operations Executive (SOE) during the Second World War.

In the Motor Museum are some of the first cars ever to roll off a production line including a Model-T Ford and a 1909 Rolls-Royce Silver Ghost, while older visitors will recognise the cars of their youth, from the first Minis and Ford Cortinas to a Jaguar E-Type and a Jensen Interceptor. Vintage film reports rerun the glory days of track tracing alongside many original classic F1 racing cars driven by British greats including the likes of Jim Clark, John Surtees, James Hunt, Jackie Stewart and Graham Hill.

As a day out for all the family, Beaulieu is hard to beat. It's not often you can choose between monorail or a 1920s London bus as your mode of transport or round a Mad Hatter topiary hedge to see the car used in the film *Chitty Chitty Bang Bang* driving by.

Its genesis harks back to 1899 when the 2nd Baron Montagu of Beaulieu drove the first motor vehicle into the yard of the House of Commons in Westminster. It was the start of a family passion that he handed down to his son, whose collection of vintage cars was first displayed in the reception room at Palace House in the 1950s. Once the gatehouse to the ancient abbey, Palace House itself was remodelled into a Victorian country house and was one of the first to be opened to the public. Today it is a fascinating treasure trove of history, art and Montagu family memorabilia.

The extensive ruins of the abbey and its surviving cloisters give a very clear impression of the architectural gem that was destroyed during the Dissolution of the Monasteries in 1538. Testament to the fact that Henry VIII should be remembered not only for his multiple wives but also as the most accomplished vandal in British history.

For budding James Bonds there is the Secret Army Exhibition. Its display cases are like a prototype of Q's workshop with maps hidden in shaving brushes and pistols in cigarette cases. During the Second World War, Beaulieu acted as a secret training ground for undercover agents later parachuted into Nazi-occupied France. Some extraordinary stories emerge, particularly of the pivotal role played by women in the war. One Beaulieu graduate was Nancy Wake, one of the Allies' most highly decorated servicewomen and once the Gestapo's most wanted person. Beat that, Jeremy Clarkson!

Uffington White Horse

Bronze Age Picasso

Looking after a horse, as any horse-owner will tell you, is a huge responsibility. But then again so is living next to one. Especially one that has been galloping across the adjacent hills for the last 3,000 years. Just ask any of the volunteers who turn out each year to help with the ongoing upkeep of the sweeping abstract lines of the famous White Horse carved into the chalk escarpment of the Berkshire Downs near the village of Uffington in Oxfordshire.

In times past, the tradition was known as 'scouring' and took place every seven years to the raucous accompaniment of festivities and general merriment, an event recorded as far back as the seventeenth century. These days the effects of weather erosion, not to mention the annual pounding of thousands of feet, means that 'Chalking the Horse' is now an annual event. Layers of weed and moss are removed, and fresh chalk added to a horse that measures 365ft from the tip of its tail to its ear and whose lines are dug into the hillside 3ft deep.

Unlike every other equine figure carved into the hills of the south of England, the modernist lines of this, the oldest of them all, could easily have been lifted from the sketchbook of a twentieth-century master. 'Picasso', it seems, was alive and well in prehistoric Britain. Even if his Bronze Age equivalents were using antler picks to create their masterpiece.

But the purpose of the White Horse is not certain, although it was unlikely to have been purely decorative as we see it today. Among its many mysteries is the question of how it was meant to be viewed. Putting aside madcap theories of alien spacecraft, it does seem strange that the best view is from the air. One theory is that the horse is a tribal symbol that can best be seen from a distance and which would have acted as a deterrent to hostile groups seeing it from afar. It may have been a totemic symbol of the tribe that lived here, a territorial marker, a fertility symbol, or a mixture of all three.

Although there are some good long-distance views of the horse from nearby roads in the Vale of the White Horse, its power and significance in the landscape are best appreciated by approaching it from the Ridgeway, the 'oldest road' in Britain, and taking a detour to the nearby Dragon Hill across the valley. The Ridgeway passes some of the best known prehistoric sites including Avebury stone circle, Wayland's Smithy – one of the country's best-preserved Neolithic burial chambers – and a series of Iron Age hill forts.

Above the horse is Uffington Castle, another ancient fortress, while to the north is the dome-shaped mound of Dragon Hill is where St George is said to have slain the dragon. From the top of the ridge there is a spectacular view into the deep coombe below, known as the Manger. This valley with no river was created by glacial meltwater, while the ice-cut terraces on its west flank are known as the 'The Giant's Stair'.

For many years archaeologists assumed the horse was created during the pre-Roman Iron Age due to its resemblance to horses on contemporary coins, which had similar 'beaked' mouths and flowing limbs. Or possibly that it was of Anglo-Saxon origin celebrating the victory of Alfred the Great over the Vikings at nearby Ashdown in 871. Finally, however, deposits analysed in the 1990s dated it to the late Bronze Age, around 1000BC.

Fountains Abbey & Studley Royal Water Garden

Piety, power and pleasure gardens

Henry VIII created them and posterity has immortalised them. Monastic medieval ruins have fared well for the heritage industry in recent times and the romantic ruins of Fountains Abbey, set off by that masterpiece of landscape design, the Studley Royal Water Gardens are the jewel in the crown.

This fusion of medieval monastic power and Georgian pleasure gardens comes together in the steep-sided valley of the River Skell in North Yorkshire, near Ripon, complete with manicured lawns, moon pools, statuary, follies and tunnels in one of those accidents of history that you would not have any other way.

It all started when some disgruntled Benedictine monks from nearby
York broke away from their monastery to found their own community as part
of the Cistercian Order. Despite some disastrous decades around the Black
Death, by the time Henry VIII made his break with Rome the monastery had
built up such significant landholdings and wealth from the wool trade to make
them the perfect target for the king's coffers. After its dissolution the abbey
was looted for building materials by its subsequent owners.

Two centuries later John Aislabie, a Tory MP and Chancellor of the
Exchequer, was blamed for the financial disaster of the South Sea Bubble.
After being briefly imprisoned and losing his seat in parliament, he retreated
to his estate in Yorkshire to lick his wounds. Politics's loss was posterity's gain
and the water gardens he created, and which were later carried forward by his
son, are a masterpiece of landscape design.

Exploring both abbey and gardens makes for an unforgettable day out. A
successful fusion of opposites on a grand scale. The abbey's medieval design
was a final flowering of pre-Gothic Romanesque architecture on an epic scale.
Strolling down its 300ft nave surrounded by soaring arches and windows,

ruined flights of steps going nowhere, eroded mouldings and grotesques, with the Perpendicular tracery of the tower stonework glowing in the afternoon sun, is a powerful experience indeed.

It is often thought that it is the abbey itself that won the estate its World Heritage status in 1986. But the citation makes clear that it is in fact the 'harmonious whole of buildings, gardens, and landscapes... which represents over 800 years of human ambition, design and achievement.' Studley Royal Water Garden is an essential element of this harmonious whole and one of the few great eighteenth-century gardens to have survived in its original form.

As well as the stupendous views across the canals, cascades and ponds to the abbey itself, must-see features of the garden include the follies (Banqueting House, Octagon Tower, Temple of Fame, Temple of Piety), the statuary (Neptune, Bacchus, Antaeus being squeezed to death by Hercules) and the eerie Serpentine Tunnel on the high path overlooking the valley, a joke by Aislabie at the expense of his more timid guests.

Lindisfarne

A holy island

Self-contained, cut off, shaped by the seas and the weather patterns that surround them, islands all have a unique character. There are warm and welcoming islands and there are cold and hostile islands, party islands and Robinson Crusoe islands, islands lapped by azure seas with palm-fringed beaches, desert islands, islands covered by ice, jungle, lava or sand, there are flat islands and there are mountainous islands.

But there are also holy islands. Few in number but spiritually charged, something about them has attracted holy men and ascetics throughout their history. One such is Lindisfarne. Tethered only by sand, mudflats and a causeway to the coast of Northumberland, its tenuous umbilical cord disappears

twice daily under the ebb and flow of the sea like a human soul precariously connected to its bodily form, liable at any moment to be swept away.

Perhaps this is the reason why it has been the home of so many saints over the centuries. One of the earliest Christian monasteries was founded here by the Irish monk St Aidan in AD635. A few decades later it was the turn of St Cuthbert, who joined the monastery as a monk, left to become a hermit and then returned as bishop. Although originally buried on Lindisfarne, where miracles were reported at his tomb, Cuthbert's body was later moved to Durham Cathedral where it became one of the most important pilgrimage sites in medieval England. His coffin, complete with seventh-century carvings and relics from the tomb, is now on display in the cathedral.

Holy Island is also where the illustrated manuscripts known as the Lindisfarne Gospels were created, probably by a monk named Eadfrith who was also later canonised. Due to the infamous Viking raids of 793 and the later invasion of the kingdom of Northumbria by the Danes, the monks eventually left the island, taking with them Cuthbert's body and the Lindisfarne Gospels, which now reside in the British Library.

Visiting the island today is to make an imaginative journey back into this medieval monastic world. Many follow the poles that mark the Pilgrim's Path over the sands from the mainland, some having walked the 62-mile route of St Cuthbert's Way from Melrose in the Scottish Borders. Chief among the island's sights are the atmospheric ruins of the twelfth-century priory requisitioned by Henry VIII during the Dissolution of the Monasteries. Its Romanesque arches frame views of the moorland and the coast where the fairy-tale silhouette of Lindisfarne Castle on its rocky ledge dominates the skyline.

The castle, which is in the care of the National Trust and has recently undergone a major restoration, was originally built as a defensive fort in Tudor times but underwent major reconstruction by the Arts and Crafts architect Sir Edwin Lutyens in the early years of the twentieth century. The nearby garden, once the garrison's vegetable plot, was created by the famous Edwardian garden designer Gertrude Jekyll.

Walking the island's perimeter, modern-day pilgrims are greeted by the sounds of curlews and oystercatchers, while seals and dolphins can be seen from the dunes. Little has changed since St Cuthbert's day.

Portmeirion Village

Wales

Nothing is at it seems. Reality seems to have split apart. Are we on a Tuscan hillside or an estuary in Wales? Is this a film set or a bizarre, multi-coloured yellow, pink, blue and green holiday village with domes, rotundas and towers thrown in for good measure? Who are those people pretending to be chess pieces in the central piazza? What time period are we in? Is this now or then? And if the latter, when is then? And who is this Number Six?

If middle-of-the-road certainties and architectural consistency are your thing then the village of Portmeirion overlooking the Dwyryd estuary on the west coast of Wales is probably not for you. If, however, you are an iconoclast or an architecture buff with a taste for the eclectic – Baroque, Classical, Italianate, Jacobean, Gothic, Regency, Palladian, anything in fact that is aesthetically pleasing and definitely not functionalist or Brutalist – then look no further.

Portmeirion was built over a period of 50 years between 1925 and 1975 by the mostly self-taught architect Sir Clough Williams-Ellis. Williams-Ellis – who had won a Military Cross during the First World War – wanted to demonstrate how architecture could be both beautiful and fun without insulting the surrounding landscape. His primary intention was to recreate the feeling and colour of an Italian village and the atmosphere of the Mediterranean.

During a period when beautiful old houses throughout the land were being demolished, Williams-Ellis saved beautiful period features – ceilings, facades, urns, columns, statues, colonnades – and incorporated them into his designs, so much so that the village came to be known affectionately as the 'home for fallen buildings'. There are dynamic, imaginative structures everywhere you look but all are different. The village is built around a natural amphitheatre overlooking the estuary. At its heart is the central piazza with its palm trees, fountains, blue-tiled pond, densely planted flower beds and columns supporting gilded Burmese dancers. Adjacent is the Bristol Colonnade, which once fronted an eighteenth-century Bristol bathhouse, its roof and decorative stone urns part of the Promenade which winds through the village.

Portmeirion has had some famous visitors over the years: George Harrison celebrated his 50th birthday here in 1993. But when it comes to Portmeirion even the Beatles cannot compete with the fame of Number Six. The 1960s cult television series, *The Prisoner*, starring Patrick McGoohan, tells the story of a man who attempts to leave the Secret Service but after being gassed in his apartment finds himself imprisoned in 'The Village' where everyone, prisoners and guards, are known only by their number. Anyone trying to escape never knows who they can trust. Portmeirion was the perfect canvas for the surreal storyline and memorable scenes, including a giant chess game with human pieces, are regularly re-enacted in the central piazza.

Stratford-upon-Avon

The Shakespeare pilgrimage trail

Every year thousands of literary pilgrims flock to Stratford to follow the fascinating trail of the Bard of Avon's journey from life to death. Like collecting stamps in a pilgrim passport along the famous Camino de Santiago, there are more than a few must-sees along the way. Chief among them is the house in Henley Street where Shakespeare was born and grew up, the third of eight children. Of relatively simple architectural design, constructed of wattle and daub around a wooden frame of local oak from the Forest of Arden, it would nonetheless have been a substantial town house at the time it was built. Favourite exhibits include a copy of the First Folio of his plays, published in 1623, and John Shakespeare's glove-making workshop where father and son would have worked together when Will was a boy.

Since becoming a literary mecca, it has acquired the signatures of many famous names on its walls and windows, and in its guest registry, including Lord Byron, John Keats, Charles Dickens and Alfred, Lord Tennyson. Sacrilege of sacrilege, there was once a plan by the American circus owner, P.T. Barnum, to ship the entire house, brick by brick to the United States. Happily the organisation that later grew into the Shakespeare Birthplace Trust, and which owns the house today, stepped in and the house was saved for the nation.

A few minutes walk away is Hall's Croft, the home of Shakespeare's daughter, Susannah. Nearby are the garden, artworks and exhibits that now occupy the location of New Place, where Shakespeare lived, worked and finally died in 1616. The house itself was demolished in the eighteenth century by its then owner William Gastrell, who had become fed up with Shakespeare fans staring through the windows, a crime that makes failing to sign the Beatles seem positively trivial in comparison.

The most devout pilgrims will not want to miss the farm where his mother Mary Arden was raised and which is now run as a working Tudor farm. Activities include archery, a bird of prey display and – this being Tudor times – goose herding. There's also Anne Hathaway's cottage, where William wooed his wife-to-be. Both are just a ten-minute drive from the centre of Stratford. Many pilgrims then celebrate the completion of their odyssey by catching a play at the Royal Shakespeare Theatre.

But if there is one holy of holies that no true pilgrim can miss, it is Shakespeare's tomb itself in Holy Trinity Church with its famous curse on anyone who 'moves my bones'. Although the keepers of the sacred shrine like to play it down, a non-intrusive, ground-penetrating radar image for a Channel 4 documentary marking the 400th anniversary of Shakespeare's death in 2016 suggested that the old legend of his skull being stolen in 1794 may well be true.

Whatever the truth and whether the grave robber echoed Hamlet's words at the grave of Yorick, 'Alas, poor Shakespeare!', the riddle of what happened to the bard's skull, if indeed it no longer lies in its original resting place, will probably never be known.

In which case it's tempting to hope that the famous curse came true.

Sutton Hoo Ship Burial

Final resting place of Anglo-Saxon royalty

Myth, legend and real-life history all combine in the astonishing story of the Sutton Hoo ship burial. In 1939, just a few months before the outbreak of the Second World War, a self-taught Suffolk archaeologist, Basil Brown, discovered a seventh-century Anglo-Saxon ship burial in the grounds of a Suffolk estate belonging to Mrs Edith Pretty. Mrs Pretty, who had an interest in both spiritualism and archaeology, wanted to know what lay beneath the many ancient mounds on her land and had asked Brown to help her.

The work had started the previous year when Brown discovered a small number of artefacts that suggested further investigation was worthwhile. Now, digging alongside two estate workers on a different mound, the team quickly

discovered iron rivets followed by the clearly defined ghost image of a ship measuring 89ft from bow to stern. The timbers had long since rotted away in the acidic soil, leaving behind the fossil outline of a ship.

It was a find that was later described as one of the most important archaeological discoveries in England both for the beauty and quality of the grave goods and the light it shed on an era of history from which there is little surviving documentary evidence. The mound had many of the same features as the descriptions of ship burials in the Old English epic poem, *Beowulf*, as well as the ritual burials in southern Sweden where the poem is set.

It is now thought that the ship was the burial chamber of Rædwald, King of East Anglia from about AD599 to AD625. On his death, the oak vessel, which was his mausoleum, would have been hauled up the hill from the River Deben and lowered into a prepared trench. The ruling Anglo-Saxon dynasty that Rædwald belonged to, the Wuffings, buried their dead at Sutton Hoo during the height of the kingdom's political dominance, the mounds expressing their power and status.

Now on permanent display at the British Museum in London, the treasures from the burial site include the richly decorated helmet that has become an iconic symbol of the Sutton Hoo site and of archaeology in general. The features of its ornamentation combine the eyebrows, nose and moustache of a man with the anatomy of a dragon with outstretched wings.

The Great Gold Buckle is decorated with mythical creatures including writhing snakes, birds and intertwined four-legged beasts. The ornamental purse-lid would have covered a lost leather pouch whose contents survive in the form of 37 gold coins. The quality of the artistic design and craftsmanship in all the artefacts found in the burial chamber suggest the work of master craftsmen with skills of the highest order.

Today the site has been transformed into a cutting-edge interpretation site with the help of a grant from the Heritage Lottery Fund (HLF). The project, called 'Releasing the Sutton Hoo Story', has enabled the National Trust to create an experience that helps visitors discover more about this internationally significant site and how its stories have captured the imaginations of people the world over.

Mount Stewart

'Land of Heart's Delight'

Few women (or men for that matter) have left their personality so indelibly stamped on the landscape, both inside and out, as Edith, Marchioness of Londonderry. Her legacy is the house and gardens of Mount Stewart, the Neo-classical mansion on the shores of Strangford Lough in County Down, Northern Ireland.

Although the estate had been owned by her husband's family since 1744, by the time Edith became chatelaine in 1921 it had been neglected for long periods. During the First World War, as well as her role as a society hostess, she had been both a political activist and a wartime leader, founder of the ground-breaking Women's Legion in Britain. She had also been a suffragist campaigning for votes for women.

On her arrival at Mount Stewart, she recorded in her many letters and papers, which still survive, that the house only had one bath and that it felt both damp and dark. Nonetheless she soon fell in love with its glorious views describing it as her 'Land of Heart's Delight', and began decorating the house in her own flamboyant style, full of bright colours, contemporary fabrics and unusual furniture. The latter included a lavatory in her own private bathroom disguised as a chest of drawers.

As well as her charisma and creativity, Lady Edith brought glamour, style, politics and parties to Mount Stewart. Her fame and influence attracted royalty, high society and politicians including Prime Minister Ramsay MacDonald, alongside the literary and artistic titans of the day. A place to see and be seen. She rapidly transformed not only the fabric of the house from the heavy Victorian atmosphere she inherited but also nearly 80 acres of gardens, which she radically redesigned.

Taking advantage of the unique micro-climate of the Mount Stewart estate, Edith was able to amass an unrivalled collection of rare and exotic plants from across the globe, experimenting with planting schemes based on bright colours and strong scents, a tradition that has been followed to this day with rare specimens from more than 50 countries. She believed in designs that

reflected her own idiosyncratic interests so the gardens are full of allegories and references to classical and Celtic mythology, the Italian Renaissance, Spanish gardens, heraldry and her own family.

The formal areas have a strong Mediterranean feel with spectacular inventions that include the famous Italian Garden with its Dodo Terrace, affectionately satirising the Ark Club, a group of socialites that she had founded in 1915. Edith's father, Lord Chaplin, was immortalised in the dodo sculptures and her husband as 'Charlie the Cheetah'. It was a vision that resulted almost a century later in the gardens being voted among the top ten Gardens in the world.

Mount Stewart was gifted by Edith and her daughter Lady Mairi to the National Trust, who completed a three-year, £8 million renovation of the house in 2015. Among many other family-friendly attractions, today's visitors can enjoy the mile-long red squirrel trail around the lake and gardens, home to one of the few surviving populations of red squirrels in Northern Ireland.

MUST-DO
EXPERIENCES

The Minack Theatre

Cliff-edge drama on the coast of Cornwall

The play is Shakespeare's *A Midsummer Night's Dream* and Theseus is delivering his famous speech on the power of the imagination. He describes the frenzied eye of the poet glancing from earth to heaven and giving: '... to airy nothing/ A local habitation and a name.'

Rowena Cade, who bought the Minack headland on the Land's End peninsula in the 1920s, must have been listening intently to the words of Theseus when a few years later she attended a production of the *Dream* in a grassy field a few miles inland. Its success inspired her to create an outdoor theatre on her own land. Looking down over the cliffs below her house towards Porthcurno Beach, from 'airy nothing' she created what was to become the world-famous Minack Theatre. Much of the work clearing granite boulders, constructing the banked seating, the amphitheatre and the layout of the stage, which was originally of grass, was done by Rowena Cade herself and two friends who were gardeners and craftsmen. Her intricate graphic designs and the names of early plays performed at the Minack can still be seen carved into the seats, pillars, steps and walkways.

The first production was of *The Tempest* on 6 August 1932. Lighting technology was limited to the use of car headlights to illuminate the stage. Nonetheless, the production was a great success, even garnering a positive review in *The Times*. For many years afterwards, the cast used her house to change in until the first purpose-built dressing rooms arrived in 1954. Tickets were purchased from a trestle table in the garden before the audience clambered down the steep cliff to their seats.

Perhaps the greatest challenge for the actors performing in a space so lovely is keeping the audience focused on the action and drawing their attention away from their sublime surroundings. On a summer's night when the light slowly fades and the light turns orange over The Lizard peninsula clearly visible across Mount's Bay to the east, even Oberon's magic can seem surplus to requirements. Over the years audiences have been spellbound not just by Shakespeare & Co., but also by schools of basking sharks and dolphins.

The downside of course is when the wind begins to howl and the rain to bucket down and it becomes all too easy to imagine Lear on his blasted heath. Famously, rain never stops a Minack performance assuming it is safe to continue and, remember, while rain gear and warm clothes are welcomed, umbrellas are strictly forbidden. This is a theatre after all!

Over the decades, Shakespeare has provided the backbone of the Minack's output along with regulars like Dylan Thomas and Tom Stoppard, while the musicals of Rodgers and Hammerstein and Gilbert and Sullivan (*The Pirates of Penzance* of course) have been hardy perennials as well as adaptations of local Cornish novelist, Daphne du Maurier. In recent years, many concerts have also been held at the Minack.

Few works of the imagination have moved audiences like Shakespeare's. Few audiences have had the privilege of seeing them performed in a setting more inspiring than Rowena Cade's.

Spitfire Flight

Reach for the skies!

Once upon a time only heroes flew Spitfires. But these days we can all don goggles and fighter pilot headgear to enjoy our own 15 minutes of fame shooting down imaginary Messerschmitt Bf 109s. In fact, your time reaching for the sky will be double that, 30 minutes to be precise. Longer if your wallet is fat enough.

At the Boultbee Flight Academy based at Goodwood, West Sussex, you will be strapped into the cockpit of a two-seater Spitfire Mk HF-IXe with a Rolls-Royce Merlin 66 (1750hp) engine. At 21,000ft, this legendary warplane has a top speed of around 400mph.

Everything from takeoff to landing is hyperreal. Within a few minutes of the wheels leaving the ground, your pilot will be making a 'Look! No hands!' gesture from the seat in front and asking whether you'd like to take the controls instead. 'Who, me?' 'Yes, you!' You're the one with the fighter pilot fantasies. Admit it! That was you running around the garden, arms outstretched with your young son, shouting 'Dakker-dakker-dakker' over the hedge at your bemused neighbours.

But this time it's for real. Your heart is thumping as the fields of Blighty whizz by beneath the Spitfire's legendary elliptical wings as your trembling hands nervously close around the control stick. (You certainly won't be calling it a joystick now you're a real Spitfire pilot.) Just pray the guy in the front seat isn't a fantasist like you. He did say he was an ex-Royal Navy fighter pilot didn't he?

After testing your nerve with these few seconds of madness – was that really me who made a real live Spitfire bank left? – your pilot will be back at the controls again. If he thinks you're ready for it, this is when the fun really begins. It's now that you'll find you've changed your tune slightly from your tally-ho spirit when you signed up for this over a glass of wine too many. As you prepare for your loop the loop, you'll be thanking your lucky stars that in real life there's no sign of a squadron of 109s coming at you out of the sun.

Suddenly you are pointing up at the heavens, the next diving straight into the sea over Selsey Bill. The needle on the airspeed dial spins crazily from 200 to 300mph. When you look back at the footage from the video camera capturing your every facial expression, you will see your face creasing into paroxysms of delight even as the world flips upside down and spins back on itself.

It will all end with a victory roll over RAF Tangmere, the Second World War airfield where the legendary fighter ace Douglas Bader flew from during the Battle of Britain. And suddenly, before you know it, you will be touching down once more and bouncing over the turf towards the hangar, wishing you could do it all again tomorrow. From now on, you too have performed aerobatics in a Spitfire. Maybe not one of 'The Few', but certainly one of 'the few'.

Glamping

Far from the madding crowd

The core ingredients are the same: the Great British countryside, the sights and sounds of nature, stunning landscapes, evenings around the camp fire and that blissed-out feeling of having escaped, for a while at least, the relentless commute and the daily grind. Far from the madding crowd indeed. But once upon a time, a camping holiday was not a camping holiday without one vital ingredient: canvas.

Times have moved on. Perhaps it has something to do with the evolution of the African safari. These days safari tents in the bush have morphed into boutique pavilions with designer interiors, showers and baths with hot and cold running water, beds with Egyptian cotton sheets, hot-water bottles when the nights are cold, and gourmet meals served al fresco with views over the savannah. What canvas there is comes heavily supplemented with the very best designer materials.

Back home, we have developed our own version of the luxury bush experience. It's called glamping. In place of the old-fashioned inverted 'V' kept upright by rickety wooden poles, we now prefer yurts and gers, bell tents, tipis, gypsy caravans, Airstream trailers, domes, pods, shepherd's huts, lakeside log cabins and treehouses with all the mod cons of a luxury hotel suite.

Out-and-out luxury is far from the only form of glamping. Anything that stimulates the imagination and retains closeness to nature without the need to dispense completely with life's creature comforts is all part of the Cool Camping movement. One of the best examples of the latter is to be found in Blackberry Wood, near Ditchling in the Sussex Weald, with views towards the nearby South Downs. Over time the site has evolved from a magical woodland setting with old-style pitches for old-style canvas into an

increasingly imaginative site that covers the spectrum between the old and the new. Glamping options include a 1964 Routemaster London double-decker bus, an original 1930s gypsy caravan, a converted 1965 Wessex Search and Rescue helicopter, a curvy eco-cabin and a choice of two fairy-tale treehouses, Higgledy and Piggledy.

Top of the glamping sustainability charts comes Loveland Farm, a campsite on a 6-acre farm a mile from the cliffs and beaches of Hartland Point in North Devon. The site is owned by fashion designers Jeff and Karina Griffin, and has a combination of geodesic domes and tipis complete with solar panels, eco-showers, state-of-the-art compost loos and biomass wood burners.

For top-end glamping, things don't get better than Secret Meadows at White House Farm near Aldeburgh in Suffolk. Accommodation on the organic 115-acre farm includes a combination of safari tents featuring range ovens, four-poster beds and candle chandeliers with a gypsy caravan, shepherd's hut and converted horsebox.

Kielder Observatory

Our darkest sky at night

The next time you're online, take a look at a light pollution map of the UK. The chances are you'll find that you live bang in the middle of one of those bright yellow splodges. Then have a closer look and try and find an area of true midnight black. There are not many of them but in Northumberland just a few miles from the Scottish border is Kielder Forest, home to the third largest Dark Sky reserve in the world.

At nearly 580 sq. miles, Northumberland International Dark Sky Park is protected in law from the ravages of light pollution and has been awarded Gold Tier status by the International Dark Skies Association, putting it in the same league as Death Valley and Big Bend Dark Sky Parks in the United States.

'Remember to look up at the stars and not down at your feet,' urged the late Stephen Hawking, 'Try to make sense of what you see and wonder about what makes the universe exist. Be curious. And however difficult life may seem, there is always something you can do and succeed at.' Words echoed in a more surreal context by Eric Idle's 'Galaxy Song' in Monty Python's film, *The Meaning of Life*, 'When you're feeling down Mrs Brown...'

They are words of advice that visitors to Kielder Observatory have taken to heart if the anecdotes of their reactions to a tour of the night sky through one of the observatory's powerful telescopes are anything to go by. Astronomers at the observatory tell of 80-year-olds bursting into tears at their first sight of the rings of Saturn.

It is estimated that 85 per cent of the UK population has never seen a truly dark sky. That's because light pollution follows us around, concentrating in the cities and towns where we live. For 99.9 per cent of the two million years of human evolution, apart from camp fires, the only light at night was from the stars above. When Homo sapiens emerged around 300,000 years ago, our elders and chieftains began using their interpretation of the constellations to plan big events during the calendar year. But when Thomas Edison introduced the first electric lightbulb less than a mere 150 years ago, all that changed forever.

As our cities and towns have become oceans of nocturnal light, so have the heavenly bodies disappeared from our consciousness with the result that today few of us have experienced the sense of wonder that a clear night and a truly dark sky filled with thousands of stars can bring. More people read their stars in the newspapers than know the constellation Orion from Cassiopeia or the planet Mars from Venus.

If you have ever felt a thrill of anticipation running through your veins at the thought of seeing a close-up view of a lunar mountain range or a deep space object like another galaxy, then a visit to Kielder Observatory should not be missed. The best time for stargazing is during the autumn and winter months, when the nights draw in. When the sky is at its darkest in winter the Andromeda galaxy, the nearest spiral galaxy to our own, is even visible to the naked eye.

Fish & Chips

A Great British tradition

At the beginning of most quizzes, there's usually an easy 'Starter for Ten' to calm the nerves and put some easy points on the board. And so it should be with a Bucket List. After all, if you live in Cornwall, the Scilly Isles are on your doorstep but the Outer Hebrides present a tougher ask. So here's your easy opener. What's the first thing you think of that's utterly British and utterly unmissable? The answer can only be... fish and chips!

It's always said that food or drink associated with specific countries or regions always tastes better on home turf. So haggis, neeps and tatties will inevitably tickle the tastebuds more in Edinburgh than they will in London. The same applies to Bakewell tarts, Yorkshire pudding and, yes, Cornish pasties. And it's certainly true that nothing competes with a shot of single malt atop a Scottish Munro or a pint of Guinness at a ceilidh in Cork.

That's not to say that food can't successfully cross boundaries. Chicken tikka masala is now claimed as a British national dish and fusion foods are all the rage. But the ultimate traditional dish is surely one whose origins are rooted in local produce and local traditions. Take a bow, fish and chips.

But not so fast. Culinary historians tell us that it was actually Portuguese Jewish immigrants (*Marranos*) who popularised battered fish in the sixteenth century and the chips arrived later courtesy of the Irish. Who put them together and when is marred in controversy. Some claim it was John Lees who sold fish and chips from a wooden hut in Mossley Market in Lancashire, but the first fish and chip shop was opened by Joseph Malin in Bow in the 1860s.

To taste truly authentic, many say fish and chips should be eaten within sight of the sea. And it's true that the crunch of footsteps on a shingle beach, the suck and surge of the surf, and the whiff of salt in the nostrils at the end of a day by the seaside is the perfect accompaniment to crisp batter, succulent white fish and perfectly fried, golden chips. Not forgetting, of course, a liberal lashing of salt and vinegar.

But given the length of our Great British coastline, it doesn't narrow the options that much. After all, there are around 10,500 chippies nationwide to choose from. So where will you find the ultimate fish and chips? If it's culinary excellence you're craving, you'll do no better than to check out the winners of the annual 'Fish and Chips Oscars', a competition to find the best chippy in the land, judged by Seafish, a public body that supports the fishing industry while promoting sustainability, and hosts the awards ceremony in London. But, while some do, not all previous winners pass the seaside test. It all comes down to whether you think the quality of the food is more important than the sea air, that glorious sunset, and those wonderful friends whose fingers are all over your chips before you've even had a chance to snaffle one yourself.

Isle of Arran Coastal Drive

Scotland in miniature

Highlands, lowlands, castles, mountains, lochs, glens, burns, heather-covered moorlands, prehistoric monuments, bays, beaches and the most beautiful coastal roads in the British Isles. Whatever it is you associate with the landscape of the Scottish mainland, you will find it all off the west coast on an island in the Firth of Clyde measuring just 20 miles by 10.

Often referred to as 'Scotland in miniature', the Isle of Arran contains all the elements of its big brother's most beguiling features. With a population of fewer than 5,000 souls, it is also refreshingly free of the traffic jams, traffic lights, roundabouts and roadworks, which make the average journey so different from the seductive promise of the average car advertisement. Put the two together and it is no surprise that its 56-mile coast road is considered one of the most beautiful touring routes in Britain.

The island is connected to the mainland by a 55-minute ferry journey from Ardrossan to Brodick, Arran's capital, across the Firth of Forth. On arrival, the most difficult decision you will have to face is whether to turn left or right when you leave the ferry port. Clockwise or anti-clockwise? Highlands first or Lowlands first?

Turning right and heading north from Brodick you will first pass its eponymous castle, the Victorian baronial seat of the Dukes of Hamilton and one of the island's top attractions with formal gardens, waterfalls and woodland trails. Further north the silhouette of Goat Fell, the highest point on the island, looms above the coast road while on its lonely promontory rises thirteenth-century Lochranza Castle near a village of the same name. Lochranza is said to have been where Robert the Bruce landed on his return from Ireland prior to his successful bid for the Scottish Crown. (Fans of the cartoonist Hergé will also be interested to learn that it was also the inspiration behind the castle in the Tintin story, *The Black Island*.)

Rounding the northern headland down the west coast you will find stunning views over the water to the jagged outline of the hills on the Mull of Kintyre before the landscape becomes gentler and more wooded south of the Highland Fault Line. Now the views are of rolling pastures looking out over Kilbrannan Sound and the coast where a sandstone cave is one of the many

candidates where the ubiquitous Robert the Bruce is said to have been inspired
by the antics of a persistent spider.

For those who like to combine some brisk walking with a car journey, the
south of the island has an array of possibilities, especially as the Arran Coastal
Way, which also circumnavigates the island, runs roughly parallel with the
road. At the village of Lagg, a ten-minute stroll leads to the ivy-clad ruins
of Kildonan Castle, once used as a hunting lodge by the kings of Scotland.
Another southern gem is the charmed walk to the Eas Mor waterfall and its
accompanying loch on the plateau above.

Returning full circle on the east coast again, another circular walk climbs
up through a wooded glen to reach the viewing platform for the spectacular
Glenashdale Falls with its double drop. The route then continues to the Giant's
Graves – two chambered cairns – with panoramic views over Whiting Bay to
Holy Island and its Buddhist retreat beyond.

Forest Bathing

Mother Nature's aromatherapy

Nature Deficit Disorder. This very twenty-first century illness was first described and given a scientific name by American author and journalist Richard Louv, who published a book in 2005 called *Last Child in the Woods*. This highlighted the damage being done to both the mental and physical health of children by increasing alienation from the great outdoors.

In many ways his insights were nothing new. The Japanese obviously felt they were onto something in the 1980s when the practice of *shinrin-yoku* was introduced as a health therapy and meditative aid as part of a public health programme. Translating as 'forest bathing', the idea was to persuade people to spend more time in nature, walking and meditating in woods and forests, and to make it a national pastime that would enhance health and happiness. Japan now has 48 Forest Therapy Trails with qualified Forest Therapists on hand to help soothe away the stresses of everyday life.

The health claims of *shinrin-yoku* are supported by an impressive body of scientific studies that underline its physiological and psychological benefits. Walking among trees reduces levels of the stress hormone, cortisol, while improving mood, lowering anxiety, and delivering a boost to the immune system from breathing in phytoncides, which trees emit to protect themselves from germs and insects. Phytoncides are a tree's essential oils and are made up of antimicrobial compounds.

Blood pressure is reduced more than it would be walking in an urban environment, and forest bathing also increases levels of adiponectin, a hormone that regulates the metabolism of lipids and glucose, thereby protecting against heart attack and even diabetes. One study suggests that creative problem-solving is improved by 50 per cent after three days immersed in nature with all access to modern technology removed.

But is all this science a little unnecessary. Whatever happened to plain old common sense? Any keen walker will tell you that forests and woods have a special magic. The intoxicating sight of a sea of bluebells in a woodland setting in early spring; the yellows and oranges of autumn leaves against the deep blue sky of an October afternoon; the sounds of birds in the trees and animals scurrying through the undergrowth; the play of light through the forest canopy in the early morning and the late evening. A balm to the soul, not just the head and the heart. Just thinking about it instantly calms the mind.

The National Trust has long supported forest bathing in the numerous woods and forests that it manages around the country. These include Padley Gorge on the Longshaw Estate in Derbyshire, Standish Wood in Gloucestershire on the edge of the Cotswolds, Coed Ganllwyd in a magical corner of Snowdonia, and St Catherine's Woods near Windermere in the Lake District. At the latter, in the heart of the forest, you'll find Footprint, an innovative straw bale building created as a base for people to reconnect with nature through workshops and courses. The perfect antidote to Nature Deficit Disorder.

Glyndebourne Festival Opera

Heaven? Sir David Hockney thinks so

It's a sublime summer's evening at Glyndebourne, the world-famous opera house hidden away in the sylvan folds of the South Downs. You and your party have just enjoyed a delicious picnic washed down with a glass of champagne and are gazing out over the lawns in front of the manor house towards the hills beyond. It's now that reality and fantasy begin to blur.

The real world versus the world of magic and the imagination is a theme that pervades many a famous opera from Mozart's *The Magic Flute* to Britten's *A Midsummer Night's Dream*. Glyndebourne is an opera in its own right.

Like many a classic, it comes in five acts. For the first act there is the afternoon arrival and the finding of the picnic site. (Are you tablecloth on the lawn types or picnic tables and chairs?) A relaxing stroll around the lake swiftly follows.

The second act is heralded by the adrenaline rush that follows the five-minute bell, the finding of seats and the dimming of the lights as you are swept up in a fantasy world inside the opera house itself. The staging and the costumes are the most opulent the imagination can create. These are magical worlds brought to life with all the exuberance of the most creative minds on the planet, from orchestral musicians to choreographers, costume and stage designers, lighting engineers, conductors, and directors. Oh, and I almost forgot... the opera stars themselves.

Act three – some would say this is the best of the lot but don't breathe a word to the leading lady – is the hour-and-a-half long interval when the picnic hampers are thrown open and the popping of champagne corks drowns out the outdoor oratorio of bird song in the trees.

Act four seems to fly by as the opera reaches its climax and the audience drum their feet on the floor to a chorus of 'Bravo! Bravo!' at the final curtain before smiling faces spill out onto the balconies and the crowd slowly disperses. As artist Sir David Hockney says: 'I'm sure a lot of English people think heaven might be a little bit like this. Mozart drifting over the lawn. Certainly I might.'

But without the Christie family, whose estate this is, and the inspiration of John Christie, who started the festival in 1934, none of this magical confusion between fantasy and reality would be possible. John Christie's founding vision was carried forward by Sir George Christie, who presided over the building of the new opera house, which opened in 1994, and finally into the present day by Gus Christie to whom the baton has now passed.

And finally to the last act itself. The bittersweet departure. After a last stroll around the lawns as darkness begins to fall, you finally find yourself in the outside world once more. You must forgive yourself for wondering, along with John Keats: 'Fled is that music? Do I wake or sleep?'

Foraging

Gathering food for free

It all began with Richard Mabey's seminal book *Food for Free*. First published in 1972, it is a guide to more than 200 types of food that can be gathered in the wild in Britain and explores their history and folklore, as well as how to identify them and the best ways to cook and eat them. The book was also a manifesto for a connection with nature we are in danger of losing forever. As Mabey wrote: 'The shrink-wrapped, perfectly-shaped, "hero" produce we find in our supermarkets [...] makes us reluctant to venture into woods, pastures, clifftops and marshlands in search of food.'

However, the idea that foraging started in the 1970s is not strictly true – as Richard Mabey knew only too well. In fact, it's about 2.5 million years out. Things began to change very late in the story of our species. Our long tradition of hunting and gathering gradually died out after the first experiment with farming around 2,000 years ago. In evolutionary terms, this was followed in the blink of an eye by a further disconnect from the origins of our food with the invention of the supermarket. Since then, many of us have forgotten where our food actually comes from. Hence all those startling headlines about children not realising that milk comes from cows, bacon comes from pigs and spaghetti grows on trees. Or have I got that wrong?

Although care should always be taken to correctly identify foraged foods to avoid accidental poisoning, foraging can be enjoyed in any season and in many different habitats, with roots, green vegetables, herbs, spices, flowers, fruits, fungi and nuts all on the menu. Even the seaside is a fertile source of free food with certain species of seaweed now a prized delicacy in many gourmet restaurants.

The National Trust supports the use of most of its land for foraging abundant wild food species for personal use in the belief that good foraging

reminds us that we are part of nature and can help us tame the human instinct to over-exploit. It also believes that foraging activities must be based on the principle of sustainability and that we must protect vulnerable species and habitats. The Trust is deeply concerned about the widespread gathering of fungi, particularly from Sites of Special Scientific Interest (SSSIs) and is supporting the creation of an independent Guild of Foragers while working with other organisations to develop national codes of good practice.

The Trust runs a number of foraging walks and half-day courses on its land all over the UK in partnership with local experts. Foraging for the abundant wild garlic which grows from late winter until the end of spring is particularly popular. The leaves can be eaten raw or cooked or made into a tasty soup or pesto. The taste is milder than shop-bought garlic.

Fort William to Mallaig Steam Train

All aboard the Hogwarts Express

The past is a foreign country. They have steam trains there. The sounds are
all different (you know the kind of thing – chuff chuff, clickety clack) and the
windows, the doors, the seats and the décor of the carriages all belong to a
lost world. There is a magical thrill about sitting in a vintage railway carriage
being pulled by a steam train. On a sunlit day you can even see the shadow of
the steam trail racing along beside you over the fields. All you need now is that
long piercing whistle as the train thunders into a tunnel.

Thankfully there are a number of heritage railways across the land where
steam still rules. For those of a nostalgic bent they all revive memories of
a different way of life. Of a golden age before that pantomime villain, Dr
Beeching, uprooted 6,000 miles of track (one-third of the rail network) and
closed more than 2,000 stations in the early 1960s. The result was the loss
of hundreds of branch lines whose retention would have made the transport
system of today considerably more efficient.

Happily, some survived, particularly in Scotland where the lobby against
the Beeching cuts was strongest. And today the west coast line between Fort
William and Mallaig, first opened in 1901, is one of the most popular in
Britain. Often described as one of the greatest railway journeys in the world,
the 84-mile round trip passes Ben Nevis, and through a dramatic landscape of
glens, lochs and sea inlets.

It also crosses the Glenfinnan Viaduct overlooking the Glenfinnan
Monument, erected in 1815 on the shores of Loch Shiel to mark the spot where
Bonnie Prince Charlie raised his standard in 1745. The 100ft tall, 416-yard long
viaduct is an engineering icon with 21 arches and an elegant curving line.

But far more important than all this for today's passengers is that the

viaduct is the location of one of the most memorable scenes in the film *Harry Potter and the Chamber of Secrets*. This is where Arthur Weasley's enchanted Ford Anglia, with Harry and Ron on board, flies over the Hogwarts Express after they had been left behind on their return to school. Harry tumbles out of the car but manages to grab the door and climb back in with the help of Ron.

Powerful locomotives are needed to cope with the demanding highland gradients and beautifully restored steam engines are all part of the 'Jacobite' service, which runs twice daily on weekdays between April and October with original British Rail First and Standard Class carriages. Today visitors come from all over the world to see the 'Harry Potter Bridge' from the surrounding countryside. But nothing beats a day out on the Hogwarts Express itself.

Yorkshire Sculpture Park

Art without walls

Consider this conundrum. Is the Yorkshire Sculpture Park (YSP) – which you will find just five minutes after leaving the M1 at Junction 38 near Wakefield – the world's best motorway pit stop or is it one of the world's best outdoor sculpture parks? Like art itself, it really depends on how you look at it. After five hours at the wheel in solid traffic, the former wins hands down. But if you have the time to make a day of it as a destination in itself, the latter is infinitely more satisfying. Admission is free; you only have to pay to park your car.

Opened in 1977 with just 31 sculptures, the YSP was the brainchild of Peter Murray who back then ran the postgraduate course in art education at Bretton Hall College, and who had the idea of displaying sculptures in the grounds. The art college was housed in the Grade II-listed Bretton Hall, an eighteenth-century Palladian country house, and today the surrounding 500-acre park welcomes around half a million visitors a year. Meanwhile Peter Murray CBE is Executive Director of an organisation that is one of the world's most important open-air museums.

YSP's stated mission is to 'challenge, inspire, inform and delight' by displaying the work of acclaimed international artists in a country park of stunning rolling countryside, woods and lakes. Completing this rural scene are sheep and Highland cattle interacting freely with the works of art.

The park gives a comprehensive overview of British sculpture in the twentieth century alongside internationally famous artists. These include Henry Moore, Barbara Hepworth, Joan Miró, Elisabeth Frink, Antony Gormley, Andy Goldsworthy and Ai Weiwei to name but a few. The works displayed are frequently updated and there are several indoor galleries (three of them are underground), as well as a restaurant and café in the visitor's

centre. YSP has also pioneered the commissioning and curating of numerous open-air exhibitions and events.

The popularity of the park among the artists whose work is displayed here is underlined by the fact that while the YSP has never had the money to buy artworks, many artists have donated works or made long-term loans. Peter Murray's commitment to displaying each individual work in the most appropriate setting is an important part of its appeal.

To this end the park has been restored and reinterpreted with key views, which had been lost over the centuries, opened up. Two huge lakes have also been dredged while historic features including footpaths, a classical Greek-style summerhouse and a magical shell grotto have been restored. The way the works are presented has also evolved, giving more importance to the changing light and the surrounding landscape. Both Hepworth and Moore believed sculpture should be released from the constraining walls of the gallery and the ultimate aim in Murray's own words is to site every work in a place 'where it looks like it has been there forever'.

GARDENS
NATURE &
WILDLIFE

Sissinghurst Castle Garden

'Literary-lesbian-hortico-aristocratic amalgam'

Sissinghurst is the flower-child of the memorably unconventional liaison between the writer Vita Sackville-West and diplomat Harold Nicolson who, in 1930, bought the Sissinghurst Estate in Kent and over the next three decades transformed a wasteland of into one of the world's most famous gardens. Their grandson, the writer Adam Nicolson, who with his wife, Sarah Raven, have injected new life into the estate, has memorably described it as a 'literary-lesbian-hortico-aristocratic amalgam'.

Appropriately enough, given its recent history as a revitalised working farm, the property started life as a Saxon pig farm. But a more illustrious history was waiting in the wings, first as a moated manor house and later as the rose-pink Elizabethan pile complete with courtyards, arches and tower at its centre that we know and love today. The estate was handed over into the care of the National Trust in 1967 following the death of Vita Sackville-West, but Sissinghurst is still the home of the Nicolson family to this day.

The gardens are like a theatrical performance, with each of the garden 'rooms', as the various sections are called, creating a different mood, and having their own season to shine. They were created in the 1930s by Vita and Harold, a combination of Harold's architectural planning and Vita's planting, each room being different from the last in its theme, colours and scent. The couple spent time enjoying each one when it was at its peak before moving on to another area when the flowers began to fade. As their son, Nigel Nicolson, later wrote: 'The garden was their sustained pleasure, expressive of their common attitude to nature, keeping it cool, Kentish and indigenous. Flowers should not quarrel, no more than people. They had achieved at Sissinghurst a serenity that matched their own lives.'

The White Garden

Until 1950, the White Garden was filled with roses but as they outgrew their space they were transferred to what was to become the Rose Garden. As Harold wrote in a letter to Vita: 'I have a [...] really lovely scheme for it: all white flowers. White clematis, white lavender, white agapanthus, white double primroses, white anemones, white camellias, white lilies.'

The South Cottage Garden

Warm reds and gold mark out the South Cottage Garden, which is a riot of colour in late summer and autumn. The early summer-flowering rose 'Mme Alfred Carrière', which grows alongside the wall of the South Cottage, was the first plant that Vita and Harold planted at Sissinghurst on the day their offer to buy was accepted.

The Orchard

Vita and Harold wanted the Orchard to be half-garden, half-wilderness.
Roses were planted against the boughs of old apple trees, with winding
paths mown through the long grasses. Bees buzz among the apple blossom
and make honey in the hives. The gazebo was built in 1969 in memory of
Harold Nicolson.

The Lime Walk

Also known as the Spring Garden, this is one area where Harold controlled the
design and planting. Long beds of tulips, fritillaries and hyacinths are marked
out by an avenue of pleached limes, punctuated by generous terracotta pots,
every inch bursting with colour for about four weeks.

Blakeney Nature Reserve

Sanctuary of the seals

It is one of the wildest and most pristine sections of our eastern coastline and the letters after its name only serve to underline its importance. Both an AONB (Area of Outstanding Natural Beauty) and SSSI (Site of Special Scientific Interest), the 4-mile shingle spit of Blakeney Point on the north coast of Norfolk is recognised internationally for the importance of its seal colonies and its breeding birds.

The town of Blakeney itself was once a prosperous medieval port but went into decline when its sea channels silted up. The sand bars and the shingle spit, which protects the harbour and the surrounding saltmarshes from the wilder excesses of the North Sea, attract thousands of migratory and native

birds helping to make it a favourite shooting gallery – let's be accurate, 'killing ground' – during the Victorian era.

Luckily for future generations, and the Little Terns that now call this home, in 1912 the National Trust purchased the area from Cley Beach to the tip of the peninsula to create the Blakeney National Nature Reserve – the first coastal nature reserve in Britain – protecting this fragile ecosystem for the nation. The iconic wooden Lifeboat House was added in 1922 and is now a visitor centre and acts as accommodation for the rangers, originally known as 'watchers'. From here they carry out their crucial scientific work starting at 4am in the nesting season to monitor and protect the birds.

Along with the surrounding north Norfolk coast, the reserve can proudly lay claim to be the birthplace of the science of ecology. It marked the beginning of a radical new science, which instead of focusing solely on protecting individual species, recognised the mutual dependence of all species in the larger surrounding ecosystem.

But Blakeney Point is now most famous for its mixed colony of common and grey seals. The former have their young between June and August, while the greys breed in winter, between November and January. Grey pups are born

on land with white coats and feed on their mothers' milk for up to three weeks as they triple in size and gradually shed their white fur. In 2001 just 25 pups were born but numbers have increased steadily and now Blakeney Point has the largest seal colony in England, with 3,000 grey seals.

The ranger team protect and monitor the colony. Disturbance is a major issue and can lead to abandonment or the accidental crushing of the pups by the adults, which can be fatal. For the safety of seals and visitors, the western-most mile of beach and dunes on the Point are fenced off during the breeding season. Pups are regularly counted, and any found to be seriously ill or injured are taken to the RSPCA animal hospital.

Blakeney Point is about as wild as it is possible to get in southern Britain. There are no roads and, for anyone who has tried it, the 3-mile walk (one way) from the car park along the shingle spit is an ordeal best left to athletes in training. The best way to see the wildlife is to take one of the ferry trips that run several times a day from Morston Quay.

Winkworth Arboretum

The making of a masterpiece

'It was the remarkable beauty of the valley [...] quite unspoiled, of pastoral and wooded character, patterned with hedgerows and abounding in wild flowers with gentle undulating hills on the east side and a steep slope on the west side [...] and the river stream winding between forming two lakes.'

In 1937 Dr Wilfrid Fox purchased 130 acres of woodland next to his farmhouse in the Thorncombe Valley near Godalming in Surrey. A renowned dermatologist with a passion for horticulture, he had already been the driving force behind the planting of tens of thousands of trees along Britain's roads. This had been achieved in his role as Secretary of the eccentrically-named 'Roads Beautifying Association' for which he was awarded the Victoria Medal of Honour by the Royal Horticultural Society.

Dr Fox had owned Winkworth Farm since 1918 and jumped at the opportunity to obtain the neighbouring land so he could create an arboretum where he could experiment with autumn colours on a grand scale. Back then most of the area was covered with plantations of larch and Douglas fir. Dr Fox began by planting maples, oaks and liquidambars but was interrupted by the Second World War. After his heroic return from the rescue mission at Dunkirk (aged 64), the Ministry of Supply ordered the larches near one of the lakes to be felled for the war effort. This resulted in a bowl-shaped area of cleared slope where Dr Fox subsequently focused his efforts.

Cherries, maples and azaleas were chosen for their blazing autumn displays and being an ardent fan of the *Sorbus* genus, Dr Fox also included more than 50 *Sorbus* species – including rowan, whitebeam and service. One of the problems he successfully overcame was the issue of how many of each species he should plant to achieve a dramatic splash of colour while at the same time avoiding 'hard, clear-cut lines.'

After the war ended, he expanded beyond autumn colour, planting springtime species including magnolias and flowering crab apples. Much of the physical labour required to create the arboretum was carried out by family members as well as friends and colleagues who came to visit. His granddaughter recorded that it was very hard work but great fun!

Before his death in 1962, Dr Fox donated the arboretum to the National Trust and Royal Horticultural Society. An ongoing work-in-progress, Winkworth is now home to an internationally significant collection of more than 1,000 different species of shrubs and trees, many of them rare. Its creator used plants to paint a picture in the landscape – and the best way to appreciate his work is from a distance. Viewpoints are dotted around the higher areas of the arboretum at the best locations to experience the full effect of Dr Fox's vision. These include the edge of the Magnolia Wood, the top of the Azalea Steps, the famous lakeside Boathouse and the eastern Meadow.

The Eden Project

Welcome to Planet Conservation

Look after our planet, our planet looks after you. That's the message of the Eden Project, Tim Smit's visionary recreation of a rainforest in a worked-out Cornish china clay pit. Its geodesic domes – inflated panels of triangles, pentagons and hexagons made into 300ft domes – are filled with thousands of plants and trees recreating the environmental conditions of both a tropical rainforest and the micro-climate of the Mediterranean.

The 35-acre site is a shrine to ingenuity and the human imagination filled with sculptures, play areas, vegetable gardens, restaurants and even a zip wire, all with environmental conservation, education and sustainability as their core message. The result is the world's most exotic, scent-filled, fun, interactive, imaginative and sheer mind-blowing classroom on the planet.

The world's largest indoor rainforest is home to exotic plants from cocoa pods, coffee beans, bananas and rubber plants to the red powder puff flower and the gigantic (and very smelly!) titan arum. There's also a waterfall, roul-roul partridges and Sulawesi white-eye birds, while the Canopy Walkway and its Weather Maker exhibits transport you into the hidden world of a rainforest canopy and explain why rainforests are vital to the survival of life on Planet Earth.

The Mediterranean dome is a scent extravaganza recreating the biodiversity of the temperate zones with plants from the Med itself, South Africa and California. These include olive groves, vineyards, cacti, date palms, aromatic herbs, giant lemon-like fruits called citrons as well as gnarled old cork trees and huge sprouting aloe veras. Tim Shaw's sculptures bring to life the myth of Dionysus, Greek god of the vines, and his followers, the Maenads, who dance and writhe through the vines beating drums and sounding trumpets.

The outdoor garden has more than 3,000 plant varieties and the pathways are full of hidden features including a secret garden telling the myth and folklore of plants, and a giant wooden ship set in a sea of tea leaves. The Core is the Eden Project's inspirational education and exhibition space housed under a spiral timber roof. Inside is The Seed, a gigantic seed-shaped sculpture carved from a single piece of granite in the pattern of a Fibonacci spiral – the growth pattern at the heart of the natural world.

Then there's the WEEEMan (Waste Electrical and Electronic Equipment), a giant 23ft high waste-monster constructed from thrown-out electrical and electronic equipment representing the amount the average British household throws away in a lifetime (3.3 tons). Meanwhile the huge bee at the entrance to the biomes reminds us how much we depend on our friendly pollinators. Flying above it is the Skywire, which provides the best view in the house complete with adrenaline on tap. England's longest and fastest zip wire (720 yards) reaches speeds of up to 60mph.

Stourhead Gardens

The genius of the place

Strolling around the world-famous gardens of Stourhead in Wiltshire, with its painterly views and stylised landscapes, the thought may cross your mind that you're walking not just through a garden but through a painting. All the more of a paradox if you happen to be visiting on a day when artists with easels are painting the scene in front of the lake with its view towards the Pantheon on the far bank. Deciding which came first, the painting or the landscape, can be something of a conundrum.

The answer is in fact the painting. The gardens at Stourhead were created by the London city banker, Henry Hoare, between 1741 and 1780. Hoare had travelled to Italy on the Grand Tour with his family and had returned inspired by the paintings he had seen, including those by the artists Claude Lorrain and Gaspard Dughet.

Lorrain (often referred to as 'Claude') was a celebrated landscape painter and the muse behind the 'Picturesque' movement of eighteenth-century garden design. Embracing natural topographic features as well as Gothic and Italianate influences, the movement was a deliberate rejection of classical garden design with its symmetrical layouts, parterres and geometric shapes. Hoare's intention was to consult the 'genius of the place in all', a concept made popular in a poem by Alexander Pope, which proposed that landscape designs should always be adapted to the context in which they are located.

To realise his vision, Hoare dammed a stream on his estate to create a lake. One theory is he surrounded it with landscape features and temples to represent the different stages of the journey of Aeneas in Virgil's *Aeneid*. Structures around the lake include the five-arched Palladian Bridge, the Gothic Cottage summerhouse, the Temples of Apollo and Flora, as well as the most

famous of them all, the Pantheon, designed by the architect Henry Flitcroft and modelled on the Pantheon in Rome.

Each feature in the landscape acts as a point of focus inviting the viewer to walk into the scene ahead, before this itself opens out to reveal other scenes that beckon the viewer ever onward. One popular circular walk around the grounds begins at the house and follows the terrace where Henry Hoare and his guests would enjoy carriage rides. It takes in the view over Six Wells Valley and St Peter's Pump, a fourteenth-century pumping house moved from Bristol by Hoare to mark the source of the River Stour. The walk continues past King Alfred's Tower, at over 160ft one of the tallest follies in England, and returns through the neighbouring Stourhead Western Estate.

Stourhead House itself should not be missed. It was one of the first grand Palladian-style villas to be built in England, completed in 1725. Although its appearance has changed over the centuries with succeeding members of the family altering it to suit their own tastes and the fashions of their time, the house remains a fascinating window onto the lives of the family that created this remarkable estate.

Royal Botanic Gardens, Kew

Our lives depend on plants and fungi

Yes, it's incredible to immerse yourself in those vast Victorian glasshouses and experience for yourself microclimates that mimic the most important plant ecosystems on Earth. It's incredible to wander along the Treetop Walkway, through the Arboretum, the Mediterranean Garden and the Rhododendron Dell. It's incredible to visit the waterlily pond and wander inside the Hive where the interior of a beehive is reproduced in real-time light and sound.

It's incredible to discover King William's Temple, the Temple of Bellona, the Ruined Arch and the newly restored multi-coloured dragons on the Great Pagoda. It's incredible to unravel the multiple layers of royal history behind Queen Charlotte's Cottage and Kew Palace and learn how the gardens became the 'botanical headquarters of the British Empire' during the Victorian era. It's incredible to breathe in the scents and be stunned by the vivid colours.

But most incredible of all is to discover how important the work that goes on here is. Kew is a living laboratory employing around 500 plant scientists and horticultural specialists. The core purpose of its science stems from a simple but often overlooked truth: our lives depend on plants and fungi.

Temperate House
Reopened in 2018 after a five-year restoration, this gigantic Grade 1-listed 1860s glasshouse has plants and trees from all the temperate regions of the world including some of the rarest and most vulnerable. With the threat of climate change, biodiversity loss and food security, these important plant collections underline Kew's role in safeguarding rare and threatened plants from extinction.

Great Pagoda
Kew's most visible building is the last remaining example of a series of follies commissioned by Princess Augusta (mother of George III) to reflect Kew's international credentials. Constructed in 1762, the building was originally decorated with 80 dragons that have recently been replaced after extensive research to replicate accurately their original design and vivid colours.

Palm House
Built in the 1840s to a revolutionary design using wrought iron to create a glasshouse with the dimensions of a cathedral but with no supporting columns, the Palm House is still one of the largest buildings of its kind in the world. It was designed to house the tropical plants that Victorian explorers brought back from their adventures in the tropics, many of which are now endangered or extinct in the wild.

The Hive
Beauty and science merge in this immersive installation designed by artist Wolfgang Buttress. Set in a wildflower meadow, the 55ft high structure is made up thousands of aluminium threads fitted with LED lights connected to a neighbouring beehive creating real-time sights and sounds from the activity of more than 50,000 honey bees.

Treetop Walkway

With a structure inspired by the Fibonacci numerical sequence frequently found in nature's growth patterns, the Treetop Walkway winds its way through the tops of chestnuts and oaks trees 6oft above the gardens below giving a fascinating insight into their complex ecosystems.

Princess of Wales Conservatory

Opened in 1987 by Diana, Princess of Wales, the most complex conservatory at Kew contains ten computer-controlled climatic zones with the majority of the space containing plants from the dry tropics (desert) and wet tropics (rainforest and mangrove swamps). Sir David Attenborough buried a time capsule here in 1985 containing seeds of basic food crops and endangered species. It will be opened in 2085 when many of the plants it contains could have become rare or extinct.

Wistman's Wood

A meeting with remarkable trees

Is that whispering you can hear really just the gentle stirring of the leaves in the trees? Or is some higher force trying to tell you something? Has your imagination been hijacked and is it, perhaps, no longer truly your own, now that the forest canopy is closing in around you? Or is it just that your conscious mind has temporarily relinquished control?

From the forests of the monster Grendel in *Beowulf,* to Shakespeare's *A Midsummer Night's Dream, Grimms' Fairy Tales,* Walter de la Mare's *The Listeners,* Tolkien's Ents and Harry Potter's Forbidden Forest, literature is full of reminders that all may not be as it seems when you find yourself alone in a forest. If there is a wood anywhere in the land that is likely to transport you into that Otherworld, it is Wistman's Wood on Dartmoor.

In the rational, conscious world, it can be reached by taking a brisk one-and-a-half-mile walk north from Two Bridges along the West Dart River, where you will find one of the highest native upland oak forests in Britain. In the not-so-rational world they are another thing entirely. Here Nature alongside Time – the sorcerer's assistant – has created something from another plane full of crooked faces, contorted bodies and distorted limbs. Wherever you look among these groves of twisted oaks, there are the shapes of wicked demons and mischievous elves. Here Ogham, the Celtic language of trees, is the only tongue spoken.

This is not just ancient woodland but possibly a rare survivor from a time when Mesolithic hunter-gatherers cleared many thousands of the trees on Dartmoor in around 5000BC. In fact these very oaks may be the direct descendants of trees that grew up after the end of the last Ice Age around 10,000 years ago.

Covering them, along with the granite boulders known as 'clitter', is a mantle of lush green lichens providing beards, invisibility cloaks and magic carpets for the wizards beneath. Arriving on a summer's afternoon with blue skies and fluffy clouds, its embrace feels benign and magical. But woe betide the unwary traveller on a winter's night at dusk.

Unsurprisingly many local legends are associated with Wistman's Wood. The druids were thought to have used it for their rituals and ceremonies. (How could they possibly resist?) But it was also thought to have been the home of the diabolical hellhounds of the legendary Wild Hunt, known as 'Wisht Hounds' in the Devonshire dialect, and the possible derivation of the wood's name.

As John Page, who visited Wistman's Wood in 1895, wrote: 'As he stands there in the gray light, with no trace of life visible, he may be pardoned if a feeling of something very like awe take possession of the soul, for he will almost expect to see the wraith of some Druid priest gliding along the steep hillside.'

Mottisfont Abbey House and Gardens

A rose by any other name

Ancient country houses are like windows into the lives of their former owners. And the former owners of Mottisfont on the banks of the River Test in rural Hampshire are as diverse and eccentric as any in England. A courtier to four Plantagenet kings, Augustinian canons, a Tudor statesman, a baronet who was also a first-class cricketer, wealthy bankers and a visionary bohemian – each with their own coterie of friends, including painters, writers and pioneering gardeners – have made Mottisfont the inimitable experience it is today.

Unique among English country houses, it was originally built as an Augustinian Priory (founded 1201) before being converted into a Tudor stately home after the Dissolution of the Monasteries. Later it became the country

seat of wealthy aristocrats, surrounded by lawns, walled gardens and a 1,600-acre estate. Owned by the National Trust, it is today one of those hidden gems that offers something for everyone, from history buffs and art lovers to architecture students and aficionados of *Gardeners' Question Time*. Exploring the house – it was never technically an abbey – is like finding yourself in a time machine whose controls have gone haywire, but is nonetheless capable of delivering some delightful, out-of-this-world experiences. Its unconventional history goes some way to explaining how you can find yourself at one moment in a vaulted cellarium – the giant larder of the thirteenth-century priory – and the next gazing up at the miraculous 3-D effects of fantasy Gothic architecture that covers the walls and ceilings of Mottisfont's huge drawing room.

The painter of this illusory mural was the artist Rex Whistler (said to be the inspiration for Charles Ryder in Evelyn Waugh's *Brideshead Revisited*). Whistler was a friend of Maud Russell, Mottisfont's young, glamorous owner, and a patron of the arts in the years before the outbreak of the Second World War. High up, almost out of sight on one of the walls, is a moving inscription written in tiny letters: 'I was painting this ermine curtain when Britain

declared war on the Nazi tyrants. Sunday September 3rd. R.W.' Whistler was later killed in Normandy on his very first day of active service.

Outside in the grounds, families enjoy informal picnics on the lawns surrounded by ancient beeches, horse-chestnuts, plane trees, oaks and an avenue of limes, before visiting the abbey stream and circular spring or 'font', which gave Mottisfont its name. The world-famous walled rose gardens were created by Graham Stuart Thomas, one of the most important figures in twentieth-century horticulture, and contain many varieties that would otherwise have become extinct. Mottisfont is home to the National Collection of pre-1900 shrub roses which, unlike modern species, flower just once a year and explode into a riot of colour every June.

The gardens are also planted with a mix of perennials to give a season-long display with herbaceous borders showcasing a huge variety of plants chosen for their structure, rich scent and eye-catching colours. Agapanthus, geraniums and peonies mingling with pinks, lilies and phlox in colours that range from soft blue, pink and white to purple, yellow and orange.

Farne Islands

Sir David's Attenborough's favourite wildlife site

What greater accolade could there be? Asked during a live Q&A session on the BBC's website where he would recommend visiting in the UK for those who wanted to encounter 'magnificent nature', Sir David Attenborough did not hesitate. His answer was the Farne Islands, and he is not alone. In Anglo-Saxon times they were synonymous with saints looking for salvation in nature and during the seventh century were home to St Aidan, famously followed by St Cuthbert, and later St Aethelwold and St Bartholomew. Our very own

could not be in better company. Today the Farne Islands – an archipelago of 28 islands anchored in the wild North Sea off the coast of Northumberland – are home to one of the most electrifying seabird colonies in Britain, offering close encounters with 23 species including large populations of Arctic terns, kittiwakes, razorbills, eider ducks and guillemots. They are also among the best places to see one of the nation's favourite birds, the puffin, numbering around 44,000 pairs. Every five years, the island rangers undertake a full puffin census to count these comical-looking creatures to see if the numbers have changed and make crucial decisions on how to protect them.

For sheer charisma, it's a close-run thing between the puffins and the grey seals. Male grey seals have a lifespan of up to 25 years and females up to 35 years. Grey seals feed on a wide variety of fish, squid and octopus, and – when not basking on the rocks – spend most of their time in the water, staying down for between four and eight minutes at a time and reaching depths of up to 100ft. The islands have the longest-standing history of monitoring grey seals

of any colony in the world. The work was started by the Natural History Society of Northumbria in 1952, followed by the National Trust who took over in 1970, and continues to this day.

The Farnes are also one of the top grey seal pupping sites in England, with more than 2,000 pups born every autumn. But life is tough being a seal pup. Almost a third die within a month, and half within their first year. Pups are weaned in 18 days, in which time they quadruple in weight. Abandoned by their mothers, they spend another three weeks or so in the colony before heading out to sea for an independent life. Given the right weather conditions, the seals are visited by rangers every four days and new pups marked on the rump with a harmless vegetable dye. Using a rotation of three or four colours it is possible to calculate how many pups are born, how many die, and how many 'disappear' before they are able to fend for themselves.

Peak wildlife viewing months are from May to July, when both Staple and Inner Farne are open to visitors.

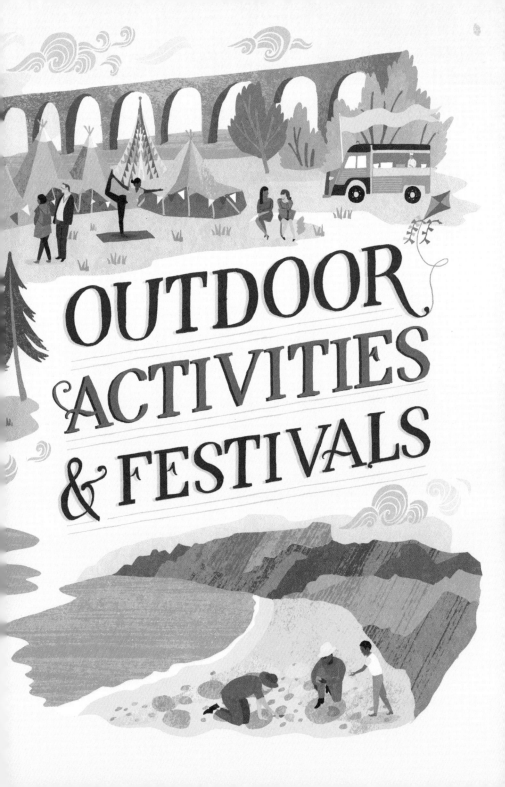

OUTDOOR ACTIVITIES & FESTIVALS

Fossil Hunting on the Jurassic Coast

Walking with dinosaurs... and Mary Anning

In 2014 a remarkable discovery was made on Lyme Regis beach. The 95-mile stretch of coastline between Exmouth in Devon and Swanage in Dorset on which Lyme Regis is located is known as the Jurassic Coast. It is the only place on the planet where time's arrow has laid bare 185 million years of Earth's geological history in the coastal cliffs and rocks. These rocks were laid down during the Mesozoic geological era between 250 and 65 million years ago. This is made up of the Triassic, Jurassic and Cretaceous periods, popularly known as the 'Age of the Dinosaurs'. It is an Area of Outstanding Natural Beauty and was designated England's first natural UNESCO World Heritage Site in 2001.

So, what was this remarkable find? The fossilised skeleton of an ichthyosaurus, perhaps? A plesiosaur, or even a flying dimorphodon? In fact, it was no more than a rough metal disc the size of a 10p coin discovered by metal detectorist Phil Goodwin. Nonetheless, it is now proudly displayed in a showcase in the award-winning Lyme Regis Museum. It is the name 'Mary Anning' stamped on one side and the date 'MDCCCX' (1810) with 'Lyme Regis' and 'Age XI' on the reverse that makes it so remarkable. For the disc belonged to a woman who in 2010, 163 years after her death, was belatedly recognised by the Royal Society as one of the ten British women who have most influenced the history of science. Mary was the greatest fossil hunter of her era and had a powerful influence on the fledging science of palaeontology, despite being largely ignored by the then exclusively male scientific establishment. Born into poverty in a house on the site of the modern-day museum, she made a living by selling fossils to wealthy visitors. She discovered the first fossil of an ichthyosaurus, a giant 30ft long marine reptile with a 4ft skull.

Today both walking and fossil hunting on the Jurassic Coast are increasingly popular activities. Among many highlights for walkers are the spectacular cliff formations at Durdle Door and Lulworth Cove where layers of rock from different geological periods have been contorted and eroded into spectacular shapes. High on the list for fossil hunters are the Fossil Forests on the Isle of Purbeck where ring shapes in the rocks outline the remains of 200-million-year-old trees and also the Ammonite Pavement on Monmouth Beach, Lyme Regis, where fossils over 2ft in diameter are preserved.

Fossil hunting is allowed along much of the Jurassic Coast as the specimens that naturally erode from the cliffs would otherwise be swept away by the sea. However, this is not the case on stretches of coastline where harder rocks mean that erosion does not naturally occur, and the use of tools such as hammers and chisels on embedded rock is not allowed.

One of the best places for fossil hunting is Charmouth Beach, although it still takes practice and luck to find a good specimen. Guided fossil walks are offered at both the Charmouth Heritage Coast Centre and the Lyme Regis Museum. But remember, you have a far better chance of finding the best fossils in winter when storms have been battering the eroding cliffs and newly exposed rocks can be found scattered along the beaches.

Walking in the Lake District

Wainwright's world

Alongside William Wordsworth in a previous age, the name of fell walker, illustrator and guidebook writer, Alfred Wainwright, has become synonymous with the Lake District. A.W., as he was known, spent 13 years walking, researching, writing and illustrating the unique series of hand-written and hand-drawn books, which later became the 'backpacker's bible' to the Lakes.

The seven volumes of his *Pictorial Guide to the Lakeland Fells*, published between 1955 and 1966, have since guided generations of fell walkers across many of the country's most spectacular summits. The 214 fells he described have become known as the Wainwrights, the Lake District's equivalent of the Scottish Munros. Having sold more than two million copies, second and third editions of the guides have been comprehensively updated by Chris Jesty, a friend and collaborator of A.W., and subsequently by writer and designer Clive Hutchby, author of *The Wainwright Companion*.

Despite the crowds that descend in high summer on the main tourist honeypots, it never takes long to escape into nature. Below is a brief summary of the geography of the fells in the same sequence as those seven famous volumes.

Eastern Fells

Dominated by the north/south Helvellyn range in the uplands between Ullswater and Thirlmere with Helvellyn (3,120ft) its highest point. To the south lies the Fairfield range. One of the best walks in the region is along the famous Striding Edge ridge approached from either the Patterdale valley or a longer walk from Glenridding.

The Far Eastern Fells

Beyond the Patterdale valley is where some of the easiest, but still stunningly panoramic, walking is to be found in an area of high moorland plateau, which at its farthest extreme at Shap Fell begins to merge into the Pennines.

The Central Fells

Characterised more by low (boggy!) ground than the airy fells for which the Lake District is most famous, the region still contains some old favourites such as the Langdale Pikes, Borrowdale and Loughrigg Fell above Ambleside.

The Southern Fells

If anywhere can be said to be the heartland of the Lakes, the Southern Fells have a strong claim if only for the simple reason that they contain Scafell Pike, which at 3,209ft is England's and the Lake District's highest peak.

The Northern Fells

Dominating the skyline north of Keswick is Skiddaw, at just over 3,000ft the sixth-highest peak in England and also one of the easiest to climb. Blencathra, formerly known as Saddleback until Wainwright himself reintroduced the older name, is another favourite.

The North Western Fells
Flanked by Borrowdale and Buttermere, the Northwestern Fells are softer and rounder than their craggier neighbours to the west, mainly due to their formation from slate rather than granite. For the best walking, head for Grasmoor, Grisedale Pike and Dale Head.

The Western Fells
Craggy and steep, the Western Fells are for the aficionados of Lake District walking and include some iconic Wainwrights like Great Gable, Haystacks, Pillar Rock and High Stile Ridge north of Ennerdale.

Kinder Scout Mass Trespass Walk

The ramblers' pilgrimage

Those grainy black-and-white photographs of a group of cheerful hikers in April 1932 give little hint of their future significance. By today's sartorial standards they look an unkempt bunch. Many are wearing shorts, long socks and what could pass for football boots as if they are off for a kick around at the local park surrounded by a gaggle of smiling supporters.

Blurry images from later that afternoon showing stick-wielding gamekeepers in plus-fours betray more of the reality of a day that has gone down in history as a seminal moment in the fight for public access to our wild spaces. For this was no random act of trespass. Although initially condemned for its 'mindless violence', in truth this was a demonstration of calm resolve to show that the wild places belong to us all, not just the few. Why should this stark but beautiful moorland be out of bounds to everyone but the privileged few.

The group of 400 ramblers, mostly from nearby Manchester and Sheffield, were determined to show that the freedom of the hills was their birthright and a welcome relief from their claustrophobic daily lives in the factories and sweatshops of the industrial north. After a scuffle with the Duke's gamekeepers on the plateau of Kinder Scout, six ramblers were later arrested and five given jail sentences of between two and six months.

One of the five was Benny Rothman, just 20 at the time, and now remembered as the patron saint of the Right to Roam movement. 'Out of about 150,000 acres of moorland and high country on our doorstep in the Peak District, less than 1 per cent was open to the public,' he recalled later. 'All the rest was owned by water companies... or by landowners with gamekeepers with sticks and dogs, and some with guns. We felt we just had to do something to gain access for all, to force ourselves to be heard.'

The sacrifice was worth it and was quickly followed by a protest rally of more than 10,000 ramblers at nearby Winnats Pass, Castleton. The Right to Roam movement had been born. As an act of civil disobedience, Kinder Scout was one of the most successful in British history. It contributed significantly to the campaign for the creation of our National Parks and National Trails and finally to the Countryside and Rights of Way (CROW) Act enacted in 2000.

Today, following the route of the main group of protestors feels like an act of pilgrimage to anyone who loves walking and the outdoors. On paper the 8-mile route can seem quite easy, but beware, the weather can close in quickly and the terrain underfoot is frequently boggy. Leave at least five hours for the round trip from the quarry at Bowden Bridge where the trespass began.

The brooding moorland of Kinder Scout is not for everyone and tends to divide opinion among keen walkers. It's not known as the Dark Peak for nothing. The ascent is the first stage of the Pennine Way, one of Britain's most popular long-distance paths, but the moorland plateau that greets you above can appear bleak and unrelenting despite its stupendous views. But love it or hate it, the experience of following in the footsteps of Benny Rothman's men is a privilege indeed.

Britain's Best Scenic Trails

It all depends on your point of view

The results of research polls asking the public to rank the best views in the land are a regular staple of the travel pages of newspapers and websites. The usual suspects always crop up, albeit in a slightly different order from the previous occasion. We'd probably all agree that the summits of the three highest mountains in Britain, namely Ben Nevis (4,413ft, Scotland), Snowdon (3,560ft, Wales) and Scafell Pike (3,209ft, England), have pretty stupendous views – whether we've climbed them or not.

Multiple locations with exceptional views have been included in other sections of this book, so here we've suggested other trails on National Trust land that its rangers heartily recommend. And they should know. Some on the list are well known, some less so. Some are challenging, some less so. Which of them is the best, only you can say. It all depends on your point of view.

Long Mynd – Shropshire

The Long Mynd is a vast heather and moorland plateau in the Shropshire Hills near the English/Welsh border. A favourite of mountain bikers and free flyers – paragliders and hang-gliders – as well as walkers, it is an Area of Outstanding Natural Beauty (AONB) with panoramic views (pictured on p.126) over the Malvern Hills to the east and the Brecon Beacons to the west.

Tennyson Down, Isle of Wight

A favourite of the Victorian poet, Alfred, Lord Tennyson, this grassy downland in the far west of the Isle of Wight has spectacular views over the Needles and the Solent to the cliffs of Dorset (pictured opposite). The huge granite cross erected in 1897 as memorial to Tennyson is the highest point of the Down.

Castle Drogo, Dartmoor

Castle Drogo (pictured on p.127) on the north-eastern edge of Dartmoor was the last castle to be built in Britain. It was designed by the great architect Sir Edwin Lutyens. The Teign Gorge walk through the adjacent valley and the views over Dartmoor from beneath the castle walls are a little-known gem.

Golden Cap, Dorset

At nearly 630ft, Golden Cap (pictured opposite) is the highest point on the south coast and England's only natural World Heritage Site. Its grandstand view includes most of the western section of the Jurassic Coast including Lyme Bay, Bridport and the 18-mile sweep of Chesil Beach. Stonebarrow Hill is a great starting point for 25 miles of footpaths around the Golden Cap estate with an old radar station housing a National Trust information point.

Seven Sisters, East Sussex

Chosen as a default screensaver of Microsoft Windows software, the view over the chalk cliffs of the Seven Sisters east of Cuckmere Haven in the South Downs National Park (pictured on p.129) is today famous worldwide. But don't be put off. Even in high summer the downland trails are a walker's paradise.

Glencoe, Scottish Highlands

Few experiences match the impact of seeing Glencoe (pictured above), Scotland's newest National Nature Reserve, for the first time. Known equally for its awe-inspiring views and tragic past, Glencoe is a place of history, wildlife, adventure and myth. The glacier-carved slopes of the reserve include eight Munros and a delicate ecosystem of moorland and birch woodland.

Pen y Fan and Corn Du Circular Walk

Wild Welsh wonderland

You certainly aren't the first and you definitely won't be the last. So there has to be a very good reason why each year more than a quarter of a million pairs of boots trek to the summits of Pen y Fan and Corn Du in the Brecon Beacons. It could, of course, be the fact that they are the two highest summits in southern Britain at 2,907ft and 2,864ft respectively. Or perhaps it's down to those phenomenal views across central and southern Wales to the Severn Estuary and beyond. On a clear day, the Cambrian Mountains, the Black Mountains, the Gower Peninsula, Herefordshire, Gloucestershire and even Somerset on the far side of the Bristol Channel are all visible.

Or then again, perhaps it's the magnetic allure of the landscapes themselves with their stark beauty and fearsome reputation as a training ground for Britain's Special Forces. The surrounding National Park covers more than 500 sq. miles from Abergavenny in the east to Llandeilo in the west with Pen y Fan, flanked by Corn Du and Cribyn, dominating the skyline for miles around.

Folklore, prehistory and real-life tragedy also have their part to play in the appeal. Clearly visible from the summits of both peaks below the steep, once glaciated, northern escarpment is the lake of Llyn Cwm Llwch. A doorway to an enchanted island on the lake was said to open on May Day each year with travellers being told by the fairy inhabitants they must take back nothing but memories. Needless to say – humans being fallible – the rule was broken and a flower was stolen. The door to the Otherworld has not been opened since.

Meanwhile, back in the supernatural world of prehistoric times, cairns on both peaks conceal Bronze Age burial chambers. A bronze brooch and spearhead were unearthed on Pen y Fan when it was excavated in 1991. On a sadder but still mystical note, the tragic death in the mountains of five-year-old

Tommy Jones is commemorated by an obelisk on the ridge above the lake to mark the spot where he was found. In the summer of 1900, Tommy became lost on the mountains and his body was discovered only after a local gardener's wife saw it in a dream.

Although the rewarding 4-mile Pen y Fan circuit from the Pont ar Daf car park is along well-maintained upland paths, it should only be attempted with the best equipment and navigational aids after checking the forecast for bad weather warnings. The effects of cold, heat, rain and wind are all magnified in a mountain environment.

To avoid the crowds but still enjoy epic views, try Cribyn to the east while nearby Cwm Sere, Cwm Oergwm and Cwm Cynwyn are serenely quiet valleys in the central Brecon Beacons with much less challenging terrain and views that are arguably just as impressive. For a gentler amble, head to the Upper Tarell Valley, which runs from Libanus to Storey Arms. There are also plenty of meandering walks through ancient woodland where you can enjoy views of Craig Cerrig-Gleisiad and Fan Frynych.

Water Wilderness

Paddle your own canoe

All is silence save the muted splash of your paddle and the gurgle beneath your bows as you surge forwards under the arching trees above. It's early on a summer's morning and the play of light on the surface of the water is bewitching. You've already spotted both a kingfisher and the rare sight of an otter scuttling along the riverbank. Gazing down into the water, the riverbed is clearly visible as fish dart silently, this way and that.

Whether it's a kayak or a canoe you're paddling, both can help you forge a powerful bond with the natural world and a liberating sense of individual freedom, while the view from the water brings a new perspective on both the wildlife and the surrounding land. Anyone who is reasonably fit can master the basic strokes and learn to manoeuvre and turn in a short time.

The locations below are all managed by the National Trust where you can join a group or hire the boats and kit you'll need for your own adventure. When approaching wildlife, never get too close, keep the noise down and always move on after a few minutes.

The Fowey estuary, Cornwall

The wooded creeks of the Fowey estuary are perfect paddling country or you can head upriver towards Lerryn, Lostwithiel and Pont Pill. Kingfishers, otters and, if you're lucky, a pod of dolphins are all possible sightings.

Salcombe Bay, Devon

Paddle along the Salcombe estuary to discover secret beaches and soaring cliffs. Singing Paddles, a licensed canoe operator on the Salcombe estuary, runs tours in all seasons using Canadian canoes and the National Trust has created a downloadable paddling guide to the estuary.

Studland Bay, Dorset

This glorious slice of natural coastline on the Isle of Purbeck has a 4-mile stretch of golden, sandy beach, with gently shelving bathing waters and views of Old Harry Rocks and the Isle of Wight.

Stackpole, Pembrokeshire

Stackpole is an exceptional landscape and nature reserve on the Pembrokeshire coast. Launch your kayak at Stackpole Quay and paddle along the coast to discover sandy beaches and coves.

Aberdaron, North Wales

Introductory kayaking sessions run from Aberdaron beach using single seat and tandem sit-on-top kayaks, which are easy to paddle and very stable. The local wildlife includes sea birds like puffins and Manx shearwaters, as well as seals and porpoises.

Derwent Water, Lake District

As well as the stunning Lakeland scenery of the surrounding Borrowdale valley, the sheltered bays are excellent for spotting wildfowl, while red squirrels are often seen in the surrounding woodlands. If you're very lucky, you may spot an otter. The lake supports the healthiest remaining population of Britain's rarest fish, the vendace.

St Abb's Head National Nature Reserve

Cliffs, seabirds, divers and geology students

With its sheer cliffs, offshore stacks and narrow gullies, St Abb's Head on the east coast of Scotland is one of the most stunning stretches of the Berwickshire coastline. Only 5 miles east of Eyemouth on the A1 after it crosses into Scottish Borders country north of Berwick-upon-Tweed, it is famous for its cliff walks and the thousands of seabirds that nest here every year in early summer.

But that's not all. Take the sea itself for example. As you enjoy a bracing walk along these epic cliffs, keep an eye out for dolphins, minke whales and seals. But we're not just talking about how things look from above the cliffs. Due to its excellent 'viz', as divers call the distance, you can see underwater, the colours and shapes of its underwater landscapes are like a 3-D Disney epic. (Nemo, are you out there?)

They include kelp forests, walls covered in soft coral, tunnels, gullies and a huge diversity of marine life, including everything from Arctic wolf fish to Devonshire cup corals. All these have made the site legendary in diving circles. One of its most famous features is Cathedral Arch, which rises nearly 30ft from the seabed and measures 20ft across at its base, its surfaces densely packed with dead man's fingers and plumose anemones. On a clear day, with shafts of sunlight illuminating the scene like theatre lights on a stage, underwater photo ops don't get much better.

But let us return to the surface. In fact, let's jump 300ft above the surface and take a walk across the headland from Pettico Wick to Horsecastle Bay where you will find yourself above a deep valley – quite possibly alongside a class of earnest-looking geology students. This is the St Abb's Head fault line where the secret ingredient of this compelling landscape is revealed. For while today the green fields surrounding Mire Loch are a walker's paradise, back in

the Ancient of Days – that's 400 million years ago to you and me – this whole area would have been a fiery furnace of molten lava.

To the west are sedimentary rocks laid down when a wide ocean separated Scotland from England. As the American continent (with Scotland attached) gradually moved towards Europe, these rocks were pushed up into mountains and squeezed into the folds that are now so dramatically on display along the Berwickshire coast. Meanwhile to the east are the lava flows that resulted in the spectacular coastal scenery we see today – both above and below the water.

Which brings us back to those charismatic seabirds that flock here in early summer safe from predators attacking their eggs or chicks. Guillemots and razorbills crowd tightly together on the ledges of offshore stacks while puffins use crevices in the cliff face to lay a single egg out of sight. Kittiwakes, meanwhile, build grass and mud nests on the sheer cliff faces while fulmars nest higher up on grassy ledges or in round crevices such as at Hope's Heugh. Shags and herring gulls prefer the low, flat rocks for nesting and roosting especially near Black Gable and Horsecastle Rocks.

Stackpole Estate

Welsh wanderings

Pembrokeshire is justly famous for its sinuous 186-mile Coast Path. To walk it is to surrender yourself to the subtle art of wandering, careless of both time and destination. Opened in 1970, it was the first National Trail in Wales and runs from St Dogmaels near Cardigan to Amroth near Tenby. Its three major headlands – St David's, St Ann's and St Govan's – jut into the Irish Sea like pincers on a sclerotic claw, its twists and turns concealing numerous creeks, bays, estuaries, lakes, lagoons, beaches, coves and woodland valleys.

One of its most beautiful sections is around the limestone cliffs of Stackpole Head, which takes in both Barafundle Bay – regularly voted among the best beaches in the UK – and its equally enticing neighbour, Broad Haven South. In an act of remembrance carried out by Oscar-winning director, Danny Boyle, portraits of the fallen were etched into the sand at Broad Haven South on the centenary of the 1918 Armistice before being washed away by the tide.

Stackpole Estate itself dates back to before the English Civil War and its landscape is a unique mix of the natural and the man-made. Inherited through marriage by the Scottish Cawdor family – descendants of the Thane of Cawdor of Macbeth fame – the 100 acres of lakes, which are today known as the Bosherston Lily Ponds, were created by the damming of three limestone valleys as a ornamental backdrop to their magnificent country seat, Stackpole Court.

While the house itself was demolished in 1963 after being severely damaged by troops stationed there during the Second World War, the ponds are famous for their water lilies, which carpet the water surface during June,

and can be enjoyed close-up from the boardwalks that extend into the lakes. The estate is also a haven for wildlife such as bats (nine of the UK's 18 bat species live at Stackpole), kingfishers, herons and a small population of otters, which can best be seen from the famous Eight Arch Bridge built in 1797 to connect Stackpole Court to the sea.

For birdwatchers, Stackpole Head is a great destination to see thousands of guillemots on the cliff ledges during the spring breeding season, as well as large numbers of choughs, razorbills and even a few puffins. Peregrine falcons and gannets can also be seen diving offshore, while schools of bottlenose dolphins are regularly spotted.

This stretch of coastline is also one of the best places in the UK to enjoy sea sports such as coasteering and kayaking. Coasteering, an adrenaline-fuelled adventure sport combining swimming with cliff jumping and rock traversing, was invented on the coast of Pembrokeshire, which is now home to expert guides who ensure high standards of safety along with the best equipment and the most thrilling locations.

The South West Coast Path Challenge

Beaches, lakes and coastal wonderland

Is it strange to feel emotional about a coastal footpath? After all, a path is just a meandering trail of flattened grass across clifftop meadows here, a rocky roller-coaster leading around coves and inlets there. It can be a muddy tunnel under arching groves of sycamore and oak, a gap between hedgerows, or even just footprints on a sandy beach, soon to be wiped away by the incoming tide.

The answer can only be a resounding 'No!' because every year thousands of walkers and runners express their love for the South West Coast Path (SWCP) by voting with their feet during the annual October Challenge. Funding for the path from official bodies has been in sharp decline in recent years and so a charity partnership between the South West Coast Path Association and

the National Trust has been set up to inspire people to support the path. The Trust owns a quarter of the land that the SWCP travels through and half of the money raised goes to National Trust projects.

An estimated nine million people walk at least a section of the path every year and it is currently the longest of the 16 National Trails in England and Wales. It stretches 630 miles from Minehead in Somerset to Poole Harbour in Dorset, following the north and south coasts of Devon and Cornwall by way of the Land's End and Lizard peninsulas, before ending at the eastern end of the Jurassic Coast in Dorset.

Along the way it rises and descends around 115,000ft, nearly four times the height of Mt Everest, and passes through some of the most beautiful coastal scenery in the whole of the UK. Hardly surprising then that it is regularly ranked as 'Britain's Best Walk', and among the most beautiful and popular in the world. Opened in 1978, in 2018 it celebrated its 40th birthday as a waymarked National Trail.

The idea of the Challenge is for volunteers to walk, run, jog (perhaps even hop if they have a mind to) as many miles of the trail as possible to help raise money for essential maintenance work, which, on average, costs £1,000 a year for every one of its 630 miles. While all volunteers are encouraged to design their own walks and challenges, each year the organisers come up with a series of events that showcase the SWCP's incredible diversity. These include everything from night-hikes to history and nature walks, and from trail running challenges to foraging rambles.

Events in recent years have included an evening torchlight walk to the top of Golden Cap in Dorset, the highest point on the Jurassic Coast, and a *Poldark* walk in period costume along the West Penwith peninsula north of Land's End where Winston Graham found the inspiration for his novels and where parts of the BBC TV series were filmed. Ross and Demelza would surely have approved.

Lewes Bonfire

Fire and mayhem on the streets of Sussex

Outside a war zone, nothing compares with the undiluted assault on the senses of 5 November in Lewes. Those of a more sensitive disposition are advised to plan for an early night in with earplugs firmly inserted as far away from the town as possible. Lewis in the Outer Hebrides should just about do the trick. If, on the other hand, whizz-bangs of every shape, colour, speed and intensity are your thing, then Lewes in East Sussex is the place to be.

As well as Guy Fawkes and the Gunpowder Plot, the historical roots of Lewes Bonfire date back to the mid-nineteenth century and the cult of the Sussex Martyrs, which popularised commemoration of the burning at the stake of 17 local Protestants during the reign of Queen Mary. Or 'Bloody Mary' as the fervently Catholic monarch is more irreverently known.

Bonfire Night's central spectacle is the main procession itself made up of the town's six firework societies, as well as those from outlying towns and villages, all with their own unique costumes, banners and effigies. Each society's 'smuggler' dress reflects different 'pioneer' traditions. These include Vikings, French Revolutionaries, Native Americans, Romans, Tudors and Civil War soldiers among many others. The ear-splitting rhythms of drumming bands heighten the mood of anarchy and rebellion.

The flaming torches and crosses of the Bonfire Boys light up the night while deafening 'rookies' (bangers) deliver heart-stopping jolts to unwary bystanders. Political satire more than Bonfire's 'No Popery' roots inspire today's giant cartoon effigies, which are carried through the streets ready for ritual burning later in the evening. Popular victims in recent years have included Osama bin Laden, Kim Jong-un and both Presidents Putin and Trump. (Oh yes, and Boris Johnson has had his bottom singed a few times too.)

Each bonfire society proudly protects their own traditions and represents different areas of the town. The oldest societies are Cliffe – centred around Cliffe High Street at the bottom of the town – and Lewes Borough who carry a flaming 'Monster Iron Key' representing the freedom of the streets granted to 'Borough Boys and Girls' every 5 November. Both were founded in 1853.

Despite all this, nothing quite prepares for the bonfire displays that take place at multiple locations around the town where the effigies are burnt or – more accurately – exploded in the case of Cliffe's effigy of Paul V, the pope unlucky enough to have been elected in the year of the Gunpowder Plot. Each show easily out-guns, -bangs, -booms, -blasts, -rumbles and -roars every other fire festival in the land as the huge bonfire and firework extravaganzas light up the night.

'We won't be druv' (meaning 'We won't be driven' or in modern idiom 'Don't try telling us what to do!') is the unofficial motto of Sussex in general and of Bonfire in particular. It's a clarion call to all free-thinkers everywhere and a testament to Lewes's long tradition of individualism. The anarchic spirit of Tom Paine, the town's *de facto* patron saint and one of the founding fathers of American Independence, lives proudly on.

Cooper's Hill Cheese Rolling

You are strongly advised not to attend

Of all the eccentric pastimes for which the British are famous, the Cooper's Hill Annual Cheese Rolling and Wake – which takes place every year on the Spring Bank Holiday near the village of Brockworth in Gloucestershire – is one of the most bizarre. Risking life and limb chasing a Double Gloucester cheese down a one-in-two hill makes hurling a hard leather ball at someone 22 yards away armed with a piece of willow seem relatively sane in comparison.

The 'Wake' in the title refers to the alternative meaning of the word as 'an annual festival' rather than its more common meaning as 'a vigil held beside a recently deceased body'. Given the physical risks involved and the long list of injuries sustained during each year's event, the word seems to imply both meanings, just in case. Happily, the latter has so far not proved necessary.

While winning is seriously difficult, the objective is simple: to catch a wheel of traditional Double Gloucester cheese rolled down the hill in front of the chasing competitors. Given that the cheese can reach 70mph, the former is no easy task. OK, let's be honest, it's impossible, so crossing the finishing line first has to suffice. Popular theories as to the origins of the event – the first written record is in 1826 – suggest it began either as a pagan spring ritual or as 'payment' to maintain grazing rights on the nearby common.

There are four races (three for men and one for women) with a (theoretical) maximum of 15 runners taking part in each race, although in past years as many as 40 have taken part. Entry is on a first-come, first-served basis, so the start line at the top of the hill is a frenzy of testosterone-fuelled pushing and shoving until the Master of Ceremonies announces: 'One to be ready, Two to be steady, Three to prepare (as the cheese is let fly) and Four to be off.'

It is now that the carnage begins, with the competitors running, jumping, slipping, sliding, jostling, cartwheeling and sometimes catapulting into the air as they launch themselves downhill cheered on by a huge crowd of spectators, who these days come from all over the world. A much-quoted description by a previous roller sums up the event to perfection: 'Twenty young men chasing a cheese off a cliff and tumbling 200 yards to the bottom where they are scraped up by paramedics and packed off to hospital.'

Health and Safety concerns have inevitably had to be considered and in recent years there has been no official organiser so that no one can be held responsible in the event of serious injury. Both entering and watching is, after all, entirely voluntary. Instead warning signs read: 'you are strongly advised not to attend'. Not that anyone appears to take much notice.

In 2018, champion cheese roller, Chris Anderson, broke the record for the highest number of cheeses (22) won during his 14 years of racing. Sadly, he doesn't like Double Gloucester cheese. So he donates his winnings to charity instead!

Boutique Music Festivals

Boho without the grunge

Take your pick from these two dictionary definitions of the word boutique: (a) a small shop selling fashionable clothes or accessories; (b) a business serving a sophisticated or specialised elite. Both are equally appropriate as the defining characteristics of one of the UK's most popular summer pastimes in recent years: the boutique festival.

Put these together with some definitions of a festival and you have a spot-on summary of the genre. 'A period of celebration at an organised series of concerts and talks for a specialised elite wearing fashionable clothes typically held

annually in the same place' will do very nicely to describe Port Eliot, Latitude, Larmer Tree, Byline and Wilderness to name but a few.

Music we can take as read but many have their own theme within a theme. At Port Eliot the emphasis is on literature and creative writing, at Byline it's independent journalism, at Wilderness it's music, art, theatre, comedy, conservation and the outdoors.

So what's the difference between a boutique festival and Glastonbury, Reading and the Isle of Wight for example? Size is one thing. They are smaller and more manageable even though their prices are hefty. Families with children feel safer with plenty to amuse and occupy kids of all ages. There are fewer displays of drunkenness that can mar the bigger festivals. The headline bands are more alternative, the supporting bands more indie and the environment less grungy. They are also more quirky. Latitude is famous for its flock of pink sheep while Wilderness, held at Cornbury Park near Charlbury in Oxfordshire, stages a cricket match with a live Test Match Special-style commentator and a scoreboard that records the number of streakers as

well as the numbers of runs and wickets. The streakers outscore everyone. Boutique festivals are also often held in the grounds of large country estates with centuries-old trees in landscaped gardens surrounding a lake. Here you will find spas with wellbeing centres offering qigong, yoga and transcendental meditation. There are also craft stalls, antique clothes stalls, puppet-makers, bush foraging and wilderness survival classes, as well as an array of gourmet food stalls dedicated to organic and locally-sourced produce.

While different grades of camping can be found at the Glastonburys of this world, the boutique festivals make an artwork out of it. From fully-serviced areas to pull up your trailer, motorhome, caravan or Airstream (delete as appropriate) to several-hundred-pounds-a-night luxury glamping with champagne and gourmet meals on hand.

The audiences in recent years have included Governors of the Bank of England ('Was that Mark Carney wearing the eye glitter?') and even ex-PMs and their wives ('OMG! David Cameron and Samantha are right behind us in this selfie!').

But finally and most important of all, the eco-loos are just so much nicer and cleaner. Forget the headline bands. In the end it always comes down to hygiene.

Helston Furry Dance

Cornwall's rite of spring

The origins of all the best rituals are lost in the mists of time. And the Helston Furry Dance is no different. As a rite of spring welcoming the light and banishing the dark, it has few equals. Elements of paganism and Christianity, myth and legend, music and dance, are all mixed in together with a healthy splash of hedonism thrown in for good measure.

After spending the day among the crowds who flock through Helston's winding streets and cobbled back alleyways, the instantly recognisable tune played by the Helston Town Band – the thump of the big bass drum, the rhythmic rasping of trumpets, tubas and euphoniums – will continue circling and cavorting inside your brain for days to come. Flora Day is traditionally celebrated on 8 May, the Feast of St Michael, Helston's patron saint, but when this falls on a Sunday or Monday it reverts to the previous Saturday. The day revolves around four dances originally divided by social class but now, thankfully, only by age: the young and youngish (7am); schoolchildren (9.40am); grown-ups (midday); young(ish) again (5pm).

In the early morning before the crowds arrive, the town is at its most vibrant, with trailing clusters of bluebells and the green shoots of spring bamboo adorning the doorways as the excited dancers gather in front of the Guildhall. This first dance is the longest of the day with the smallest crowds and follows the borders of the medieval town.

The Hal-an-Tow, a kind of Mummer's mystery play, begins at 8.30am at St John's Bridge and is performed at seven locations around the town. Its pantomime characters (St George and the dragon, Spanish sailors, Elizabethan lords and ladies, foliage-bedecked maidens) welcome the spring and banish the winter. As its rumbustious chorus proclaims: 'For summer is a come-O, And winter is a gone-O'. Then it's the turn of the town's schoolchildren, when up to a thousand 7–18-year-olds in pristine whites take to the streets, lily of the valley pinned to their chests – right way up on the left (boys), upside down on the right (girls). The colours of the flowers in the girls' headdresses signify the school they attend.

The climax of it all is the midday dance, the men in top hats and morning suits, the women bedecked in elaborate millinery and wearing their finest, most colourful frocks. Shouts of recognition and greetings between the dancers and well-wishers are accompanied by more smiling faces than you are likely to see for the rest of the year combined. After dancing in time-honoured tradition through the houses lining the streets, the day reaches its climax on the lawns of Lismore Gardens where the dancers gyrate into a central circle, top hats bobbing along to the rhythmic strains of the band, before sharing a reviving glass with well-wishers. Participation in the dance is still by invitation only and there is no greater honour for a Helstonian than to be asked to lead the dance. To do so you must have been born in the town.

For the rest of the day and into the night, the pubs are awash with beer and good cheer. At their heart is the Blue Anchor in Coinagehall Street, famous for Spingo, its signature ale brewed on the premises, and the inspiration for many a happy, but sore, Helstonian head come the morning of 9 May.

DRAMATIC
LANDSCAPES

The Hebrides

Islands on the edge of the world

Turquoise seas? White sandy beaches? Dolphins swimming off shore? Well that's an easy one. It must be a tropical island. I'll go for the Caribbean. How about Mustique? If that's your answer, I'm afraid you've just triggered the air-raid alarm on the BBC's *QI* quiz show. Sandi Toskvig and the rest of the panellists are rocking with hilarity at your expense. Perhaps we should also have mentioned the sheer-sided, silver-grey cliffs, the towering sea stacks, the thousands of seabirds, the basking sharks and the golden eagles soaring overhead.

As well as the country's eight National Nature Reserves, the National Trust for Scotland manages more than 400 islands off its coast. Among them are

some of the most remote, beautiful and historic islands in the Hebrides, the
farthest-flung outposts of the British Isles.

St Kilda

Located on the very edge of the Outer Hebrides and uninhabited since the
final 36 islanders were evacuated in 1930, the archipelago is a UNESCO World
Heritage Site for both its natural and cultural significance – the only dual site
in Britain. Formed from the eroded rim of an ancient volcano, people lived
here for more than 4,000 years, exploiting the dense colonies of gannets,
fulmars and puffins for food, feathers and oil. Although the last of the
islanders are gone now, their homes and crofts remain, a haunting reminder
of days gone by.

Staffa

Staffa is a tiny island a few miles from Mull whose cliffs and rocks consist of
hexagonal columns, which the sea has carved into vast caverns. These include
the world-famous Fingal's Cave. The columns were formed millions of years
ago by a vast blanket of volcanic lava that spread into the Atlantic. Staffa was

almost unknown until 1772 when the botanist Joseph Banks highlighted the wild, natural beauty of the island. It soon became a must-see location. Famous visitors have included Queen Victoria, Lord Tennyson, Jules Verne, Robert Louis Stevenson and John Keats. All were enchanted.

Mingulay, Berneray and Pabbay

On the west are rugged cliffs, caves and sea stacks. On the east, green grassy slopes, bays of white sand and turquoise seas. The islands are also home to fascinating artefacts of the people who once lived here including the intricately carved Pictish stone on Pabbay, one of only two in the Western Isles. Mingulay and Pabbay have been uninhabited since 1912, and Berneray since 1980, their abandoned dwellings the only trace of the communities that once lived here.

Canna

This small island to the south-west of Skye is alive with human history. Canna is thought to have been inhabited since 5,000BC – that's 3,000 years longer than St Kilda – and now supports a small crofting community. The island was donated to the Trust by Gaelic scholar John Lorne Campbell and his wife Margaret Fay Shaw, who together amassed and researched a huge collection of Gaelic and Celtic songs, stories, poetry and a unique collection of butterflies and moths.

Scilly Isles

The islands that time forgot

They are England's last signature before the mighty ocean swallows all land for another 2,500 miles. And this charmed archipelago, 28 miles off the west coast of Cornwall, has spawned more myths and legends in a small area than almost anywhere else on the planet. Lyonesse, Avalon, Atlantis, King Arthur, Tristan and Iseult, all are associated with the Scilly Isles.

These 55 islands – only five are inhabited – were all one until around 1,500 years ago giving rise to stories of drowned islands and lost kingdoms.

At low tide Iron Age field systems emerge from the seabed, while the burial mounds of tribal chieftains – some of whom may have been brought over from the mainland to what would have been an offshore Valhalla – are dotted throughout the islands.

The Scillies have a refreshing sense of distance from the speed of the modern world, like a welcome return to a pre-digital, analogue era of history. Cars are a rarity beyond the main island, St Mary's, and each of the inhabited five have a very distinct character, each a world unto itself.

Bryher, the smallest, only 1½ miles long and a few hundred yards wide in parts, is renowned for its beautiful white-sand beaches and shallow, turquoise sea on its protected east coast. Its contrasting wild west is a magnet for Atlantic rollers, which come crashing in over the jagged rocks of Hell Bay and was the inspiration behind some of Michael Morpurgo's magical children's novels, including *Why the Whales Came* and *Listen to the Moon*.

Next door, connected by foot over the sand flats on a low spring tide, is a different world entirely, tropical Tresco. The Abbey Gardens are famous for

their exotic displays of towering palms, desert cacti, crimson flame trees, shocking-pink geraniums, tangerine-flamed bird-of-paradise flowers, lime-green aeoniums, date palms, proteas and the thousands of other plants from Africa and Asia that thrive in the islands' semi-tropical micro-climate washed by the Gulf Stream.

St Martin's and the most westerly island, St Agnes, are the most popular with young families and couples, many of whom stay at shoreside campsites and come to enjoy their beautiful and remote beaches and walking the coastal paths. Even St Mary's, where the passenger ferry RMV *Scillonian III* docks twice a day after the 2 hour, 45-minute journey from Penzance, has the feeling of a return to a quieter, kinder and less frenetic world.

Although life can be challenging for the islanders, who have had to contend with rising house prices and an economy largely dependent on tourism and agriculture, they have always remained welcoming to outsiders. Wonderful traditions survive like the World Pilot Gig Championships on the May Day Bank Holiday when six-seater rowing boats or 'pilot gigs' race between the islands. The boats are modern versions of the vessels that used to race one another to supply a navigator (pilot) for ships entering the English Channel. Whoever reached the ship first would win the contract. These days, winning the race is reward enough.

Aira Force Waterfalls

A force of nature

Height? Width? Power? The volume of water? The thundering noise? All
of the above? What is it exactly that attracts us so much to waterfalls? As an
elemental force of Nature they have much the same mesmerising power as
their exact opposite: fire. At their heart is something raw and inexplicable, both
frightening and awe-inspiring.

Aira Force begins its slow accumulating evolution in a beck on the upper
slopes of Stybarrow Dodd high above Ullswater before turning south beneath
the slopes of Gowbarrow Fell and thundering into the ravine below. Its 70ft
descent is not especially high. In fact, compared to some, it's an out-and-out
minnow. But statistics are not really the point. The appeal of Aira Force runs
far deeper, spreading and diffusing its power into the surrounding landscape
from lakeside to mountain top, and magically transforming itself as the
seasons pass.

The poet William Wordsworth, who lived just a few miles away in
neighbouring Grasmere, was unable to resists its magnetic fascination. The
poems he wrote, which were inspired by it, including 'The Somnambulist'
about the legend of the ghost of Aira Force, were a response to a life force
he could feel all around in its venerable old oak and ash trees, its beech and
willow, its lichen-covered rocks and the beings, both real and mythical, who
have inhabited this mystical spot over so many centuries.

Even today walkers in the most mundane of moods do not need much
imagination to see elfin faces gazing back at them from the knotted and
gnarled bark of the trees on the steep hillside. Beside the surrounding
pathways are the fallen trunks of trees with hundreds, if not thousands, of
coins embedded in the bark, covering their whole surface like a suit of armour.

These 'Wish Trees' are a recent revival of a tradition dating back to the 1700s when the offerings of passers-by were thought to bring them good luck.

The arched stone bridges spanning Aira Force were built in the 1840s when the landowners, the Howard family of Greystoke Castle east of Keswick, created an arboretum below the falls, planting over 200 conifers (firs, pines, spruces and cedars) and other native and ornamental trees from all over the world, including monkey puzzle trees and a Sitka spruce now 118ft high.

But the falls are just part of a wider landscape whose seasonal changes of colour and mood make it equally as alluring on an autumn afternoon or a frosty morning in winter as in high season. In the woodlands above, red squirrels have created a protective enclave against the non-native greys and the walking trails include the 4.5-mile Gowbarrow Trail, which has glorious views from the summit of Gowbarrow towards Helvellyn in the south and the Pennines to the north-east.

Cheddar Gorge

Time, weather, Bronze Age sheep and fine young cannibals

Beauty may lie in the eye of the beholder but when it comes to one of Britain's best-loved landscapes, time, weather and the movement of tectonic plates are its creator. At more than 400ft deep in parts and over 3 miles long, Cheddar Gorge is one of Britain's best-loved landscapes, a massive fissure cutting through the limestone rocks of the Mendip Hills.

The rocks themselves were laid down during the Carboniferous period more than three hundred million years ago when the landmass of what is now Britain found itself basking near the equator covered by a shallow sea. Fast forward through geological time to around a million years ago and things were looking very different.

By this time, we had moved northwards into colder climes and had poked our metaphorical heads up above the water while still remaining connected to mainland Europe. The gorge began forming during the warmer phases between the many glacial periods that have occurred since. Water from melting ice formed a river, which over time carved into the limestone rock creating the steep cliffs we know today. The Cheddar Yeo river then gradually retreated underground forming the famous Cheddar Caves.

The result was the perfect place for our ancestors to call home. Britain's oldest complete Homo sapiens skeleton, the Cheddar Man, was found in Gough's Cave in 1903 and is estimated to be 9,000 years old. But life back then was not quite the idyll one might imagine with such fabulous views from the doorstep. Vegetarian options would have been in short supply so soon after the ice had retreated and it seems these early inhabitants practised cannibalism. On a happier culinary note, there is also some evidence the caves were later used for cheese-making, as they still are today.

As the weather steadily improved the gorge was grazed with flocks of sheep, resulting in the trademark limestone grasslands on its slopes that are so popular with walkers today. One of the consequences of the decline of local sheep farming has been that scrub and trees have started to smother the landscape, shading out the rare plants and animals that lived here. Since the late 1980s, the National Trust has been working to push back the invasive woodland allowing the light-loving rarities like the Cheddar pink, the Cheddar whitebeam and the grayling butterfly to survive and hopefully increase.

All this hard work is carried out by National Trust rangers, Somerset Wildlife Trust, and an army of volunteers backed up by a flock of Bronze Age sheep introduced from the Scottish island of Soay. The species is a primitive ancestor of the present-day domestic sheep and, along with a herd of feral native goats, ensures that the features that make Cheddar Gorge such a special place survive for generations to come.

Gower Peninsula

Space – the final frontier

Space, glorious space. OK, so Gower may not be *the* final frontier. And it's certainly true that more than a few people have boldly gone this way before. It's just that if every harassed commuter on a rush-hour train suddenly spilled out beside you onto one of its glorious beaches, you would barely even notice their presence. The annoying habits of your fellow human beings simply wouldn't matter anymore. Because, well, there's just so much… space.

Visiting this enchanted peninsula jutting into the Bristol Channel halfway along the underbelly of Wales is as near as you're likely to get to a return to a long-lost youth. And you won't need the *Starship Enterprise* to get you there either, just a beaten-up van with pink flowers painted on the side will do very nicely thank you. And don't forget the surfboard.

Alongside the long-forgotten hippy in your heart, the clichés are all here. The south coast of the peninsula is awash with vast white-sand beaches and panoramic bays, rocky causeways, spectacular cliff walks, ancient woodland, epic surf breaks and secluded inlets. And even if you were a geeky kid, in love with birdwatching and wildlife, the north coast is as beguiling a jigsaw puzzle of saltmarsh, mudflats and tidal ditches as you'll find anywhere in the country. Quite why, in 1956, Gower became the first part of Britain to be designated an Area of Outstanding Natural Beauty (AONB) is a mystery no one can fathom!

Rhossili Bay

Rhossili Bay's epic 3-mile beach is overlooked by the Old Rectory, believed to be the most photographed house in Wales, standing in magnificent isolation overlooking one of the most beautiful beaches in the world. A National Trust holiday cottage, it is the most popular on its extensive portfolio. Visible on the beach at low tide are the remains of the *Helvetia*, a ship wrecked in 1887. From the top of Rhossili Down, the highest point on Gower, much of the peninsula is clearly visible, as well as views across the sea to West Wales, Lundy Island and the North Devon coast.

Three Cliffs Bay and Oxwich Bay

Routinely listed among the best beaches in Wales alongside Rhossili, Three Cliffs Bay is a spectacular shoreline of expansive beach, tidal pools, dunes, saltmarsh and its three signature limestone cliffs. Further east, Oxwich Bay's 2½-mile stretch of pristine sandy beach backed by dunes and woodland is overlooked by Penrice Castle – a view like the cover from an Enid Blyton adventure. Between them lies Penmaen Burrows with its Neolithic burial chamber, Norman ringwork and medieval church.

North Gower coast

The quiet north Gower coast with its dunes, saltmarshes and mudflats is a tranquil place for quiet contemplation, birdwatching and walking. Along with nearby Whiteford Burrows, it is an internationally important feeding ground for wading birds and wildfowl. Llanmadoc Hill, site of an Iron Age hill fort, has wonderful views across Gower itself and to the sea beyond.

Giant's Causeway

In the footsteps of giants

There are two competing explanations as to how the 40,000 or so hexagon-shaped basalt columns, which spill out into the sea from the coast of County Antrim in the far north of Ireland, came to be there. The first is that about 60 million years ago, volcanic activity sent molten basalt bursting through fissures in the chalk bed above to create a lava plateau. The subsequent cooling and cracking created the columns that lead like stepping stones into the sea.

The second is that they were made by the giant, Finn MacCool. Anyone who has visited the Giant's Causeway, walked the magnificent coastal paths and seen for themselves Finn's boot lying among the rocks at Port Noffer – it measures in at a quietly colossal size 93.5 – will be in no doubt whatsoever.

The story of what happened goes like this. Back in the days when giants roamed the Earth, Finn had a Scottish neighbour called Benandonner

who lived in what is now Fingal's Cave on the island of Staffa in the Inner Hebrides. Challenged to a fight, Finn built a causeway all the way to the home of his rival but on seeing the even more gargantuan size of his opponent beat a hasty retreat back home to County Antrim. His reputation was saved by his quick-thinking wife Oonagh, who threw a blanket over Finn and told the pursuing Benandonner to keep the noise down or he would wake the baby. On seeing the size of his opponent's offspring and believing he would be no match, Benandonner took off back to Scotland, destroying much of the causeway as he went.

The Giant's Causeway has been a UNESCO World Heritage Site since 1986 – the only one in Northern Ireland – and is managed by the National Trust. As the only World Heritage Site in Northern Ireland, Giant's Causeway is very busy in spring and summer. To help protect it and see it at its most

spectacular, visit in winter when the wind and sea lash the extraordinary landscape. The Visitor Centre was the result of an international architecture competition. Dublin-based architects Heneghan Peng won the £18.5 million commission to design the building, which has glass walls, a grass roof, state-of-the-art interactive displays and 360° views of the coast. It has subsequently won many prestigious awards for design innovation and sustainability.

But if your head and your heart are still battling it out trying to decide which explanation is correct, sign up for the Cliff-top Experience, a guided five-mile walk from the ruins of Dunseverick Castle along the cliffs high above the causeway and ending at the Visitor Centre. Along the way you will also see other features in the landscape related to Finn MacCool – his trusty steed, a camel turned to stone, the Giant's Gate and the Giant's Eyes. And if you're still not convinced, you're probably a lost cause.

Housesteads Fort, Hadrian's Wall

Murder most foul, fast food and flushing loos

Poirot, where were you when the Roman Empire needed you most? In the 1930s, a team of archaeologists dug up two skeletons (a man and a woman) from under the floor of a tavern in the Roman village outside Housesteads Fort on Hadrian's Wall in Northumbria. One (the man) had the tip of a dagger embedded in his ribs.

Solving one of the world's oldest murder mystery cases would have been a breeze for the great detective. But, sadly, both skeletons disappeared during the Second World War. So while the truth behind this grisly event will never be known, a treasure trove of material about life in Britannia is still being found at Housesteads (then known as Vercovicium).

The Romans, for example, were the first to bring what we now know as 'fast food' to our shores, with tasty street dishes being sold from stalls in the nearby village. Isicia Omentata – very similar to the modern burger and found in the famous Roman cookbook, *Apicius* – was served to the garrison's soldiers. Its ingredients included minced pork, pepper, wine and fish sauce – and sounds a lot tastier than many of today's offerings.

Construction of Hadrian's Wall began in 122AD and took 15,000 men six years to build. Its 73 miles (80 Roman miles) joins Wallsend in the east with Bowness-on-Solway in the west. *Game of Thrones* author George R.R. Martin had the idea for his fictional Wall around the Seven Kingdoms after a visit in 1981. The adjacent Hadrian's Wall Path shadows its undulating route through the Northumbrian countryside. Housesteads was one of 15 forts as well as intervening watchtowers built along the length of the wall to keep the marauding Pictish tribes to the north at bay. In this it was largely successful, although this posting on the northern border of the Roman Empire would have been a tough one for the garrison. Nonetheless, the soldiers were very well looked after by contemporary standards. There was a bathhouse with a steam room and also an underfloor heating system, known as a hypocaust.

Even the mechanics of bodily fluid disposal gain a certain fascination after nearly 2,000 years have passed and Housesteads has some of the best-preserved Roman loos in Britain. Personal privacy was clearly not a priority as the continuous row of open-plan lavatory seats makes plain. But in a triumph of Roman engineering, the loos did actually flush. At least they did when enough rainwater had collected in the tanks outside. A hot, dry summer at Housesteads would have been a fetid affair.

An obsession with building walls is not just a modern phenomenon. Empires and nations whose borders have felt threatened by their neighbours have been in the business of wall-building for millennia. The only difference is that there was never the slightest chance that the barbarian tribes of the first century were going to pay for it.

RAINY
DAYS

Afternoon Tea
at The Ritz

A rainy day in paradise

The rain is falling steadily now. The two of you huddle together and put your heads down against the wind that is blowing down Piccadilly. The reflections of the streetlights are beginning to soften and smear across the paving stones when a passing bus sends water splashing over your shoes. You both scream, and then laugh, in resigned acceptance.

But suddenly the scene changes. A doorman in top hat and tails, red waistcoat and gleaming gold buttons is ushering you up the steps and through a revolving door as you emerge into another world. Is this a film set or a time warp? Glancing around the foyer you note the regal furniture, the mirrored walls, the busts, the garland wreaths in lavish gilt stucco, the reds and pinks of the Regency-style flocked wallpaper.

And now you are shaking off the last of the outside world as you hand over your coats to a smiling cloakroom attendant and discreetly give your shoes a quick wipe to remove any signs of that splattering of muddy rainwater. After being ushered up a short flight of steps into the famous Palm Court tea-room with its chandeliers and marbled columns, you take your seats behind a crisp white tablecloth adorned with shining porcelain and sparkling silver cutlery, teapots and cake stands that look like they've been teleported from the 1930s.

There are candles on the table and the waiters, reflected in the curving wall mirrors, are moving around in triplicate. There is a bewildering choice of 18 teas, from the ever-popular Ritz Royal English (a blend of Kenyan, Assam and Ceylon Orange Pekoe) to the more exotic Dragon Pearls (Silver Needle tea from Fujian, rolled and scented with jasmine flowers).

Soon you are tucking into neatly-cut rectangles of grain mustard mayonnaise on brioche and Scottish smoked salmon with lemon butter on sourdough. By the time the teacakes and pastries arrive in their bright colours of pink and orange, melt-in-the-mouth textures and dark chocolate interiors, your sensory glands are in overload. The soothing chords of the piano wash over you above the genial background hubbub. What is that tune? Somehow it feels nostalgic, romantic. Ah, of course, 'As Time Goes By'. Perhaps Humphrey Bogart himself will drop by later, and is that Agatha Christie you can see in the corner finding inspiration for her next Poirot mystery?

But wait, what's that the head waiter has in his hand? It looks incongruous, out-of-place, as if from another age. You stare at it in disbelief. It's an iPad! And – I don't believe this – the couple on the next table are posing for a selfie. Whatever next! Raising an enquiring eyebrow at your partner, you smile and reach for your phone and motion to a waiter who is only too happy to oblige. Within seconds your beaming smiles are being Twittered, Facebooked and Instagramed to your friends around the world.

Welcome to Afternoon Tea at the Ritz, twenty-first century style.

The Tank Museum, Bovington

Home of the Caterpillar Machine Gun Destroyer

Were it not for a quirk of history, the world's largest collection of tanks might today be known as the Caterpillar Machine Gun Destroyer Museum. Either that or the WC Museum. In an effort to keep the first prototypes a secret during the First World War, the committee in charge of its development considered a number of names that wouldn't arouse suspicions about the true nature of the new war machine. 'Water Carrier' was mooted as one alternative but its acronym was considered inappropriate. Instead, the 'Tank' was born.

The genesis of today's Tank Museum in Bovington, Dorset, dates back to 1923 when the writer Rudyard Kipling suggested that more should be done to protect the damaged tanks that had been salvaged at the end of the First World War. A shed was found and the armoured vehicles that were collected here became the basis of what was originally known as the Bovington Tank Museum when it opened in 1947.

Bovington has been an army training area since 1899 and was opened in 1916 to train tank and heavy machine gun crews for combat in France. The exhibitions in today's museum tell the story of armoured warfare and the history of the tank from the First World War to the present day. The museum's six display halls and ten themed exhibitions contain more than 300 vehicles covering all the major wars of the twentieth century. One of the exhibits traces the life of T. E. Lawrence (Lawrence of Arabia), who served with the Tank Corps at Bovington and lived at nearby Clouds Hill, now owned by the National Trust.

The Tank Story Hall contains the most important tanks and Armoured Fighting Vehicles (AFV) in history with a supporting collection housed in a multimedia exhibition. Famous individual tanks on display in the hall include Little Willy. Little Willy was the prototype of the Mark 1, which subsequently became the world's first tracked armoured vehicle to enter combat at the Battle of the Somme in 1916.

Other famous tanks include the German Tiger 131, the only working example of a Tiger in the world and restored to working order at Bovington's workshops after being captured by the British during the Second World War in Tunisia. Tigers were heavily armoured with powerful weapons and gained an aura of invincibility when rounds from a 75mm artillery gun bounced off the side of one when fired a distance of just 50m. Chief among the modern tanks on display is Challenger 2, Britain's most recent frontline tank, which saw action in both the Balkans and Iraq, and played an important role in the capture of Basra by British Forces.

Rain or shine, there are regular outdoor displays of tanks in action in the Kuwait Arena where visitors can watch both veteran and modern tanks being put through their paces with accompanying thundering engines, smoke, explosions and expert commentary.

National Marine Aquarium

Window on the oceans

We're all looking for the best and most creative ways to take time out. Recreation, after all, should be just that. Re-creation. As well as the sheer fun of finding ourselves up close and personal with some of the most bizarre creatures on the planet, recent medical studies have shown that aquariums can influence wellbeing by helping people to relax, reduce stress levels and improve moods. The perfect definition of re-creation.

The National Marine Aquarium (NMA) in Plymouth, Devon, a conservation charity, is divided into a series of zones representing the different marine ecosystems of our oceans. A visit begins with a series of tanks that replicate the underwater environment of neighbouring Plymouth Sound. Alongside is a panoramic view of the real thing so that visitors can fully appreciate the huge number of fish species and invertebrates, including sharks and rays, on their own doorstep.

Twelve miles south of Plymouth is one of the finest examples of an offshore reef in British waters and the tanks in the Eddystone Reef exhibit – featuring the UK's largest single-tank viewing panel – are home to shoaling mackerel, bass, pollock, bullhuss sharks, smooth-hound sharks, colourful cuckoo wrasse and many more.

Bizarre species of jellyfish, including the upside-down jellyfish, inhabit the Ocean Drifters display, while the Atlantic Ocean exhibit – the largest single tank in the aquarium and the deepest in the UK – is famous for its sharks. These include a 9ft lemon shark, sand tiger sharks and nurse sharks as well as rays, barracudas, tarpon and jacks. Moving around the display in three dimensions means you can walk underneath the tank (great for spotting nurse sharks) and find the best views of a Second World War Walrus Seaplane replica donated by the RAF.

The Biozone celebrates the creative miracle of biodiversity with a stunning display of exotic species including clownfish, lionfish, seahorses and a giant Pacific octopus. In keeping with the aquarium's mission to demonstrate the

importance of conservation, it also underlines the fragility of underwater ecosystems and how human behaviour can have a huge impact, not just on single species but the ecosystem as a whole.

The Great Barrier Reef is the aquarium's ultra-colourful sign-off with more than 70 species of fish and a demonstration of the vital role coral reefs play as biodiversity hot spots. Along the way you will also pass the Laboratory where scientists monitor the health of the aquarium's many underwater habitats and work on breeding programmes and coral cultivation.

Piscatorial star-spotting is all part of the fun with visitors encouraged to discover individual personalities and understand the threats each species face. Resident superstars include Penny the lobster, Denzel the boarfish, Cornelia the wreckfish, Krishna the spiny lobster and smooth-hound sharks, Stella and Stanley. And don't forget Friday the green turtle!

Down House – Home of Charles Darwin

Where one man changed the world

There are museums and then there are living museums. As an example of the latter Down House, Charles Darwin's house in Kent where he lived with his wife and family for 40 years between 1842 and his death in 1882, is in a league of its own. The house itself has been faithfully restored to the way it was when the Darwins lived here, using old photographs, the recorded memories of his children and many original artefacts which were returned to Down House after it became a museum in 1929.

The central attraction is Darwin's 'Old Study' where he wrote *On the Origin of Species,* one of the most revolutionary scientific books of all time, detailing his ground-breaking theory of evolution by natural selection. Darwin chose the room – which is actually quite small – for its practicality and the cold-light conditions that he preferred for his scientific work.

His rectangular Pembroke writing table and baize-topped worktable are windows onto the day-to-day life of a scientist who changed the way we see the world, scattered with scrolls of paper, maps, quill pens, pocketbooks, letters, glass-stoppered bottles, insect specimen jars, dissection tools and other scientific paraphenalia. Nearby is his wheeled, mahogany-framed horsehair armchair.

Almost every piece of furniture is original and there are dozens of the great man's possessions, including some dating from his time at sea. Touchingly, the basket of his beloved fox terrier, Polly, still remains tucked away in a corner while Darwin's life on HMS *Beagle*, the ship in which he famously circumnavigated the globe as a naturalist from 1831 to 1836, is brought to life by a replica of his cabin.

The house also conveys a strong sense of family life with the wooden slide on which the children would come down the stairs prominently on display. Contrary to the traditional image of Victorian parents, Charles and his wife Emma were very tolerant of the hijinks of their large family. Darwin recorded in one letter that the children were behaving in a riotous manner 'jumping on everything and butting like young bulls at every chair and sofa'. They would also play cricket on the upstairs landing and throw lead darts at one another from behind wooden shields.

The gardens, flowerbeds and walkways have also been restored to their original plan. It was here that Darwin made revolutionary discoveries about the reproductive behaviour of plants and developed many of his theories of evolution and natural selection. Several of his experiments are recreated in the grounds. Visitors can also follow the Sandwalk, his 'thinking path', a sand and gravel track on the edge of the property where he would walk every day.

The heated greenhouses are planted with the same plant specimens, including orchids and carnivorous plants, that Darwin cultivated for his botanical research projects. Much to the delight of visiting children, the guides like to tell the story of how he would demonstrate the remarkable digestive powers of Venus flytraps by feeding them toenail clippings!

Addresses

Addresses

Picture Credits

© Alamy/ LatitutdeStock: p10; Alamy/ John Prior Images: p12; Alamy: Mark Zakian: p13; Alamy/ Mohana Anton Meryl: p17; Alamy/ Steve Hawkins Photography: p18; Alamy/ David Levenson: p19; Alamy/ Paul Grover: p22; Alamy/ Prisma by Dukas Presseagentur GmbH: p23; Alamy/ Eye35: p24, 31; Alamy/ Steve Taylor ARPS: p25; Alamy/ Fabio Reis: p26; Alamy/ Brian Lawrence: p27; Alamy/ Westend61 GmbH: p32; Alamy/ Britpix: p45; Alamy/ Universal Images Group North America LLC: p46; Alamy: Russell Hart: p56; Alamy/ PBP Galleries: p59; Alamy/ Simon Dack: p61; Alamy/ AT StockFoto: p63; Alamy/ Kevin Nicholson: p64; Alamy/ Alex Thomson: p65; Alamy/ Nagelestock.com: p67; Alamy/ Travel Scotland/ Paul White: p68; Alamy/ Elizabeth Leyden: p69; Alamy/ Vytenis Malisauskas: p77; Alamy/ FotoZone: pp80–81; Alamy/ Ian Lamond: p79; Alamy/ Ian Dagnell: p96; Alamy/ Peter Phipps/ Travelshots.com: p102; Alamy/ Steve Speller: p103; Alamy/ Charles Bowman: p105; Alamy/ Helen Dixon: p107; Alamy/ Paul Weston: p126; Alamy/ Loop Images: p131, 157; Alamy/ Andrew Gillies: pp138–139; Alamy/ Beren Patterson: p148; Alamy/ Paul Cox: p149; Alamy/ Michael Bracey: p150; Alamy/ Nick Turner: p152; Alamy/ Malcolm McDougall Photography: p154; Alamy/ Westmacott: p155; Alamy/ Loisjoy Thurstan: p156; Alamy/ Ashley Cooper Pics: p162; Alamy/ A-Plus Image Bank: p163; Alamy/ Lebrecht Music & Art: p164; Alamy/ Scottish Viewpoint: p165; Alamy/ Ashley Chaplin: p166; Alamy/ Ashley Cooper: p167; Alamy/ Way Out West Photography: p168; Alamy/ Joshua Wainwright: p169; Alamy/ Sebastian Wasek: p173; Alamy/ Andrew P. Warmsley: p188; Alamy/ Tony French: p191; Alamy/ Beeta Moore: p192; Alamy: Andrew Payne: p194, 197; Alamy/ Image Broker: p195; Alamy/ Mauritius Images GmBH: p196; Alamy/ Peter Conner: p198.

© Getty/ De Agostini Editorial: p21; Getty/ Matt Cardy/ Stringer: p158.

© Glyndebourne Productions Ltd/Sam Stephenson: p72

© National Trust Images: p127; NTI/ Richard Bradshaw: p143; NTI/ Andrew Butler: p29, 50, 52, 85, 86, 87, 92, 93, 94; NTI/ /Mike Calnan/James Dobson: p35; NTI/ Joe Cornish: p40, 41, 42, 112, 113, 114, 137, 181; NTI/ Arnhel de Serra: p43, 99; NTI/ James Dobson: p38, 175; NTI/ Rod Edwards: p90; NTI/ Jo Hatcher: p128; NTI/ Tom Harman: p125; NTI/ Derek Harris: p70; NTI/ Paul Harris: p120, 122, 133; NTI/ Trevor Hart: p74; NTI/ Neil Jakeman: p108; NTI/ Chris Lacey: p36, 37, 39, 53, 146, 177, 187; NTI/ John Malley: p171; NTI/ John Millar: p134, 180, 184, 186; NTI/ John Miller: p95, 129, 140, 143, 144, 172, 174, 175, 178; NTI/ Justin Minns: p48, 88; NTI/ Clive Nichols: p100, 109, 110, 111; NTI/ David Noton: p130, 179; NTI/ Faye Rason: p147; NTI/ David Sellman: p15; NTI/ Ben Selway: p141, 142, 182–183; NTI/ Pete Tasker: p123; NTI/ Simon Tranter: p101; NTI/ Ian Ward: p89, 91, 115; NTI /Emma Weston: p14; NTI/ Andreas von Einsiedel: p51.

© Shutterstock: p151.

Index